Say Yes to
TOMORROW

DALE EVANS ROGERS

WITH FLOYD W. THATCHER

Say Yes to TOMORROW

Fleming H. Revell
A Division of Baker Book House Co
Grand Rapids, Michigan 49516

© 1993 by Dale Evans Rogers and Floyd Thatcher

Published by Fleming H. Revell
a division of Baker Book House Company
P. O. Box 6287, Grand Rapids, MI 49516-6287

Printed in the United States of America

All rights reserved. No part of this publication may be reproduced, stored in a retrieval system, or transmitted in any form or by any means—electronic, mechanical, photocopy, recording, or any other—without the prior written permission of the publisher. The only exception is brief quotations in printed reviews.

Library of Congress Cataloging-in-Publication Data

Rogers, Dale Evans.
  Say yes to tomorrow / Dale Evans Rogers with Floyd W. Thatcher.
      p.   cm.
  Includes bibliographical references.
  ISBN 0-8007-1696-5
  1. Meditations I. Thatcher, Floyd W. II. Title.
BV4832.2.R616 1993
242—dc20   93-29464

Unless otherwise noted Scripture quotations are from the New Revised Standard Version of the Bible, copyright 1989 by the Division of Christian Education of the National Council of the Churches of Christ in the USA. Used by permission.

Scripture marked TEV is taken from the *Good News Bible*—Old Testament: Copyright © American Bible Society 1976; New Testament: Copyright © American Bible Society 1966, 1971, 1976.

Scripture marked NEB is taken from *The New English Bible*. © The Delegates of the Oxford University Press and The Syndics of the Cambridge University Press 1961, 1970. Reprinted by permission.

Scripture marked NIV is from the HOLY BIBLE, NEW INTERNATIONAL VERSION ®. NIV®.Copyright © 1973, 1978, 1984 by International Bible Society. Used by permission of Zondervan Publishing House. All rights reserved.

Scripture marked JB is from THE JERUSALEM BIBLE, copyright 1966 by Darton, Longman and Todd, Ltd., and Doubleday and Company, Inc. Reprinted by permission of the publisher.

Scripture marked *Phillips* is from the *New Testament in Modern English* by J. B. Phillips, 1958.

Scripture marked KJV is from the King James Version of the Bible.

CONTENTS

A PERSONAL WORD TO OUR READERS

On a calendar that graces the Rogers's kitchen are these words by an anonymous author:

Take time to think, it is the source of power.
Take time to read, it is the foundation of wisdom.
Take time to play, it is the secret of staying young.
Take time to be quiet, it is the opportunity to seek God.
Take time to be aware, it is the opportunity to help others.
Take time to love and be loved, it is God's greatest gift.
Take time to laugh, it is the music of the soul.
Take time to be friendly, it is the road to happiness.
Take time to dream, it is what the future is made of.
Take time to pray, it is the greatest power on earth.

As we have looked up at these words day after day, the wisdom of this unknown author has expressed our deepest feelings. Let's face it—sometimes in today's world it is hard to say *Yes* to God for our todays and our tomorrows and for all that comes our way.

When we listen to the evening news at six and ten and hear all of the bad things that have happened, it is easy to become depressed and think that God has given up on us and our world. And the daily newspapers—even the so-called comic sections—don't make it any easier to believe anything good ever happens.

For example, in November 1992 a news item datelined Atlantic City, New Jersey, carried the headline: "Unattended Kids a Problem in Casinos." The lead line read, "Melissa leans against a casino wall, looking crumpled, tired and scared. She is nine years old." The writer then briefly describes the scene. It is midnight, and Melissa is waiting for her mother to finish a gambling spree. A security guard has been keeping an eye on her for two hours while trying to locate her mother. "My mother's in there and I want her," the little girl says, her brown eyes welling with tears. "I want to go to our room."

And just a month later, the newspapers released the story of a couple who had gone to Mexico on a vacation for over a week and had left their two little girls—nine and four years old—home alone to shift for themselves.

Yes, it seems that all news worth printing is bad news. Children are neglected and abused, car thefts have reached an all-time high, and in many places it isn't safe to walk the neighborhood after dark. But the message we need to hear loud and clear is this, "God is still in charge!" Our world has been beset with evil since the beginning of time, but as Christians, we know that with the death and resurrection of our Lord the battle against the bad news of sin and evil has been won for all time.

With Christ in charge of our lives, we can say *Yes* to today and *Yes* to tomorrow. And we can say *Yes* to all of God's wonderful gifts. The apostle Paul beautifully expressed who and what we are:

> In all these things we are more than conquerors through
> him who loved us, [and we are] convinced that neither

death, nor life, nor angels, nor rulers, nor things present, nor things to come, nor powers, nor height, nor depth, nor anything else in all creation, will be able to separate us from the love of God in Christ Jesus our Lord.

[Rom. 8:37–39]

With promises such as this, you and I *can* make a difference! God's provisions and gifts for a rich, full, and rewarding life are ours. Now, let's accept and use those gifts to make this a better world—a place where God's love is clearly seen and felt.

Yes, puzzling things happen to Christians—death takes loved ones; people disappoint us; we are hurt and suffer reverses. But we can say *Yes* to all of our tomorrows and move ahead boldly and with confidence because of these electrically charged words of Jesus, "In the world you will have trouble. But courage! The victory is mine; I have conquered the world" (John 16.33 NEB).

1

Say Yes to
GOD'S GIFT OF TOMORROW

For yesterday is but a dream,
And tomorrow is only a vision;
But today well lived makes every
yesterday a dream of happiness,
And every tomorrow a vision of hope.

It was New Year's Eve, and the temperature hovered
at forty-two degrees below zero. Eighteen thousand
United States Marines were poised for battle on the front
lines in Korea opposite one hundred thousand hardened
and fanatic Communist troops.

At midnight the Marines celebrated the New Year by
dining on a ration of cold beans scooped out of tin cans
while standing alongside their tanks. One of the newspaper correspondents attached to this advance unit

11

observed a big, burly Marine, his clothing and beard frozen stiff, eating his beans with a trench knife.

Sidling up to the stoic Marine, the newspaper correspondent asked, "If I were God and could give you one thing you'd rather have than anything else in the world, what would you ask for?"

After a few thoughtful moments and with no noticeable change of expression, the Marine answered, "I would ask you to give me tomorrow."[1]

That stark Korean scene reminded us of another army that over three thousand years ago was camped along the eastern banks of the Jordan River on the level expanse of the Plains of Moab. Across the rapidly flowing river was a formidable foe that was firmly ensconced within walled fortifications that had withstood bandit attacks and invading armies for centuries.

While we don't have a first-person report by trained observers, it is not hard to imagine the mood of the people in that Israelite camp. For long, hot, weary, and dreary years they had bivouacked in the lonely stretches of the vast Sinai wilderness because their fathers and grandfathers had refused to obey the Lord and by faith occupy the land promised long before to their ancestors. The years since their stubborn decision had been bitter times of pain, heartache, and waiting. But they had learned their lesson, and God had given them a second chance. The cloud by day and the pillar of fire by night had guided them in the Sinai and north past Mount Hor to their point of entry to their Promised Land across the Jordan and opposite the ancient city of Jericho.

We don't know the precise route they took, but we do know that it stretched out to approximately one hundred miles of rugged country and mountainous terrain. It was a hot, dusty, and perilous trip with hostile peoples along the way. It had to have been a relief to pitch their camp in sight of Jericho and Canaan even though they knew their future would be full of the unknown and obvious danger.

It doesn't take much imagination to picture what was probably going on in the mind of the commanding general of those Israelite forces. Although well past mid-life and advancing rapidly into that stage irreverently called "old age," Joshua doubtless carried a vivid picture of that scene more than forty years before when he and Caleb risked their lives for what they believed to be the truth, in obedience to the Lord's instructions. After spying out the land, ten of their compatriot covert agents pessimistically insisted that the Israelites were no match for their Canaanite enemies—to invade Canaan would be suicide, God's instructions and promises to the contrary. Only Joshua and Caleb spoke firmly in favor of launching the invasion. It was a bitter moment when the other ten spies had their way.

And I'm sure it wasn't hard for Joshua to relive the scene in which an unruly mob threatened to kill him and Caleb simply because they advocated doing what God had told them to do. Yes, those had been long and lonely years, but now—tomorrow—they were to break camp, cross the Jordan River, and move into their long-promised land that flowed "with milk and honey."

Joshua could at that moment say *Yes* to his tomorrow with all of its unknowns because God had assured him that he would be with his people and they would succeed. The days, months, and years of lonely waiting would soon be history. At the same time, Joshua undoubtedly remembered the details of the majority report of the other ten spies even though forty years had dragged by since that infamous day. The report pictured the Canaanites as a formidable foe, and their heavily fortified, walled cities would be impossible to take. The report had insisted that there was no way the Israelite army could subdue the giants who would be arrayed against them. And by comparison they saw themselves as mere grasshoppers.

But things were different now. Even with the waters of the Jordan at flood stage, they could say *Yes* to their tomorrow in confidence that God would see them across that barrier because he had promised to be with them. It was this same God who had engineered the escape of their fathers and grandfathers from Egyptian slavery. It was he who had guided them across the Sinai wilderness in safety to the sacred mountain where many years before Moses had been confronted by God in the burning bush. And it was God who, in spite of their bouts of rancorous disobedience, hadn't given up on them and would now—tomorrow—escort them into their Promised Land. What a glad day that would be!

Believe me, as I have moved into those years beyond the time known as mid-life, I somehow find it easy to identify with that cold Marine in Korea as he looked out across the shell-pocked no-man's-land and with General Joshua as he stared at the distant palm trees on the western side of the Jordan. There may be much about what is going on around us that is discouraging and seems impossible to handle, but ours is a God of the impossible. I am confident that as we place our faith in him, he will see us not only through today but through all of our tomorrows as well.

At the same time, though, I must confess to being puzzled by the depressingly negative attitudes that seem to plague so many people today—even Christians. It appears to be increasingly popular to concentrate on the dark side of life, to hang crepe and moan about everything that is wrong with the world. It is true that much of what dominates our news is horribly depressing—inner-city riots, looting, child abuse, abuse of the aged, scenes of hunger and starvation in third-world countries, and senseless violence.

All of this, accompanied by the carping diatribes of the noisiest of our politicians, is almost enough to plunge any sane person into the black abyss of gloom. Certainly, there is no denying the agonizing difficulties that plague us all from time to time. Yes, there is evil in our world, but to stop there, I believe, is to leave God entirely out of our calculations.

It is likely in the midst of all this that you have discovered, as I have, that present in every crowd are those who parrot the hackneyed notion that life was better and sweeter "in the good old days." It's strange that as we grow older we tend to glorify the past as we remember it. That old nostalgia virus seems to be highly contagious. I'm sure most of us can at times identify with a humorist, whose name escapes me, when he said, "Nostalgia is like a grammar lesson: we find the present *tense* and the past *perfect*."

In our better and more thoughtful moments we know beyond all doubt that though the past is terribly important, it most certainly was not *perfect*. And, yes, memory is essential to our health and wholeness, but that is just one side of the coin. The apostle Paul spoke to the other side when he urged his Christian friends in the Roman colony of Philippi in northern Greece to put the past behind and stretch or strain forward toward life ahead. I believe this was his way of telling them and us that even though our world may seem askew at times, we can say *Yes* to tomorrow with confidence that God will be with us at all times.

The late Dr. Paul Tournier, noted Swiss psychiatrist, gave us this profound insight in one of his lectures, "Life is not a stable state, but a rhythm, an alternation, a succession of new births."[2] Indeed, for the person whose faith is firmly anchored in the Lord, every tomorrow offers the opportunity for "a succession of new births." And for the Christian there is no room in this rhythm of tomorrows for the depressing gray and black clouds of doom, gloom, and pessimism.

Without a doubt, one of the most influential persons in my own Christian pilgrimage is Dr. Norman Vincent Peale, who for many years was the senior minister of New York's historic Marble Collegiate Church and who, even as I write this, is celebrating his ninety-fourth birthday. In one of Dr. Peale's sermons he speaks of Jesus Christ being "as fresh as tomorrow morning's newspaper. He is everlastingly new and gives us newness of life." For Dr. Peale "Christianity is the religion of the new." Then he adds that as we follow Christ and the advice the apostle Paul gave his Philippian friends, "We will stop saying gloomily that things are getting bad and that we haven't seen the worst," and we will come to see that "Christianity is the religion of the getting better."[3]

That kind of talk rings the bell! After all, as Christians we have a long and rich heritage. Our God is indeed the Creator and Sustainer of our vast universe and everything and everyone in it. As a matter of fact, the writer of the Gospel of Matthew gives us the marvelous assurance that our heavenly Father knows each of us intimately and values us greatly. And with this kind of Good News tucked safely into our awareness, we have no cause for dismal pessimism and, certainly, no reason to be concerned about our tomorrows. Instead, we can claim the future with pragmatic and hardheaded optimism because *God is in charge!*

Many years ago at a retreat for the Hollywood Christian Group at Forest Home Conference Grounds high in the San Bernardino Mountains of southern California, our mentor, Dr. Richard C. Halverson, who was at the time the Associate Minister of the First Presbyterian Church of Hollywood, encouraged and urged us to keep on keeping on in our Christian walk and witness in spite of the temptations that confronted all of us as professional actors and entertainers in the Hollywood scene. Then, as now, we were faced with the moral, economic, and spiritual crises that plague and threaten our society. Dick urged us to be mindful daily that Jesus Christ is the Captain of our faith and the Source of our serenity, strength, and hope. And even now as I'm reminded of that particular event, those times, and Dick's counsel, I find it very reassuring that he is taking that same message into the hallowed halls of the United States Senate in Washington as he ministers to our nation's political leadership in his role of senate chaplain.

So as we persist in our faith during all of our todays and claim with confidence our tomorrows for God, we know that there is no stage in life when we are free to coast or drift. This is most definitely not an option for us as everyday Christians whether we're in our twenties, our forties, or our eighties.

Dr. Frank C. Laubach was a great Christian hero of a generation ago. Dr. Frank spent his life as a missionary and literacy expert. He and his associates were instrumental in opening the door to a new life by teaching thousands of people to read who otherwise would never have had a chance. He was also a gifted translator, and I like the way he translated those wonderful words of the apostle Paul found in his perceptive letter written to the Christians in the Roman province of Galatia. This is the way it reads, "So let us not grow tired of doing good. When the times comes, if we do not lose heart, we shall gather a good harvest." And Paul's next words seem to speak incisively to late twentieth-century Christians of all persuasions, "So let us do good to all men [people] whenever we have a chance. *Let us do good especially to those who belong to the family of our Christian faith.*"[4] There is just no room in those words for the kind of judgmental bickering and pharisaical criticism of our fellow Christians that we sometimes hear and see in the press and on television.

My spirits have always been buoyed up and made to soar by the words of the ancient psalmist, who in a moment of noble inspiration—possibly after absorbing the exquisite beauty of the scarlet and gold eastern sky at sunrise—gave us this positive affirmation,

> This is the day of the Lord's victory;
> let us be happy, let us celebrate!
>   [Ps. 118:24 TEV]

Yes, our todays and tomorrows are meant for celebration—they are God's special gifts to us and are ours to use creatively as we live for the Lord and for his people wherever they are in today's world.

There is a little stone plaque hanging in our kitchen that was sent to us by our dear friend Dr. Lloyd Ogilvie, insightful writer of many wonderful books and the gifted preacher on the "Let God Love You" television program. The plaque reads, "Living each day as if it were our only day makes for a total life lived at full potential." Each time I read this sagacious message I am reminded that my goal as a Christian is to live every tomorrow at full potential. And I'm also reminded that while I can't do this on my own, I have a heavenly Father who is in charge of my every tomorrow.

In a moment of high inspiration the writer of Isaiah assured his readers through all time that

> Those who hope in the LORD
>   will renew their strength.
> They will soar on wings like eagles;
>   they will run and not grow weary,
>   they will walk and not be faint.
>   [Isa. 40:31 NIV]

It seems to me that as we make our way through these exciting and eventful years that close out the twentieth century and prepare for the wonders God has for us in the twenty-first, we will find it inspiring to tap the wisdom of another psalm writer who thousands of years ago wrote,

> Great is the LORD, and greatly to be praised;
>   his greatness is unsearchable [beyond our ability
>   to understand].
> The LORD is gracious and merciful,
>   slow to anger and abounding in steadfast love.
> The LORD is good to all,
>   and his compassion is over all that he has made.
>   [Ps. 145:3, 8–9]

Over and over again the writers of the Psalms express profound confidence in the unfailing goodness of the Lord and assure us that we can trust him implicitly not only for our todays but for our tomorrows as well. Admittedly, in our hurry and rush and frantic striving to make some sort of sense out of today's high-tech and computerized world, it is easy to lose touch with the kind of a God whom the psalmists knew and felt in their pastoral environment. There is so much about modern life with its hustle and bustle that tends to rob us of that intimate sense of God's presence. Consequently, it seems that all too often we find it easy to forget that God does indeed feel compassion for everything and everyone he has made. Unlike what happens so often with modern computers, God is never "down"; he is always there!

In reflecting further on these words from the psalmist, another scene comes to mind in which Jesus was looking out across the hills and valleys of Galilee, and his eyes apparently took in the vast panorama of vineyards and grain fields in which flocks of colorful birds were feeding. The scene inspired Jesus to say, "Look at the birds of the air; they neither sow nor reap nor gather into barns, and yet your heavenly Father feeds them." And then he added, "Consider the lilies of the field, how they grow; they neither toil nor spin"—and yet God cares for them (Matt. 6:26, 28).

A spectacular illustration of God's meticulous care can be seen each winter along the colorful coast of central California just a couple of hundred miles north and west of our home in the high desert. Each year in early October the large, colorful, orange and black Monarch butterflies begin to arrive and cluster on the eucalyptus and Monterey pine trees near the little resort community of

Pismo Beach—the terminus of their migration from points as far away as Canada.

As the chill of winter envelops their habitat in the faraway north country, these little creatures with a wingspread of not more than four inches make their way south and west at speeds of up to thirty miles an hour. And after crossing the heights of the Rocky Mountains and the Sierra Nevadas, they continue on west to the California coast and settle, layer upon layer, on the leaves and branches of the eucalyptuses and pines.

The thousands upon thousands of orange and black Monarchs transform those trees into colorful and fluttering masses of wings. Tourists and nature lovers flock to this sensational scene and watch in wonder by the hour. Then in late February the little Monarchs begin to leave their central California sanctuaries and head east and north to their homes in the far north, somehow sensing the arrival there of spring and warm weather.

Is all of this just an accident of nature? I don't think so for one minute. Rather, I believe that these delicate little creatures are guided through their life span by a loving God who has created in them the instinct to make their annual migration south and west . . . and then months later east and north.

For me, the sight of these Monarchs is just one among many such illustrations of the loving care of our Creator-God for us and for this world of ours. With this kind of a God we can most certainly say *Yes* not only to today but to all of our tomorrows with calm confidence. With the apostle Paul we can draw on this eternal truth and begin each day with perhaps the most astounding and life-changing affirmation of all time, "I can do all things through him [Christ] who strengthens me" (Phil. 4:13).

The American Southwest provided the stage for a rugged and stalwart people during the raw and turbulent days of the nineteenth century. Among the most heroic of them was Juan Bautista Lamy, a missionary priest who in 1851 was assigned as bishop to this desert diocese with headquarters in Santa Fe. This zealous and erudite missionary bishop made a profound spiritual impact on people from the Rocky Mountains across Colorado, New Mexico, Arizona, and into old Mexico. In 1875 Lamy was elevated to archbishop. From then until his death in 1884 Bishop Lamy continued to exercise valiant and heroic influence throughout the arid vastness of the southwestern frontier. His entire career was carved out of great hardship. But Paul Horgan, the author of *Lamy of Santa Fe*, captured the vitality of this rugged and noble man when he wrote that each day Bishop Lamy "awoke a new man." Certainly Bishop Lamy was a man of his day—and of his tomorrow.

Author Henri Nouwen expressed the idea of Christian expectation in this brief sentence from his book entitled *The Genesee Diary*, "An important part of the spiritual life is to keep longing, waiting, hoping, expecting." These words are a modern extension of the apostle Paul's thinking when he wrote,

> This one thing I do: forgetting what lies behind and straining forward to what lies ahead, I press on toward the goal for the prize of the heavenly call of God in Christ Jesus.
> [Phil. 3:13–14]

And in this pressing on process it comes through loud and clear that Paul lived each day in a way that would make Christ and the Christian faith attractive.

In a little book published many years ago by Grace

Cathedral in San Francisco, an unnamed writer left
behind this prayer:

> Let me be so strong that nothing can disturb
>   my peace of mind.
> Let me look on the sunny side of everything
>   and make my optimism come true.
> Let me be just as enthusiastic about the success
>   of others as I am about my own. . . .
> Let me wear a cheerful countenance at all times,
>   and have a smile ready for every living
>   creature I meet. . . .
> Let me be too large for worry, too noble for
>   anger, too strong for fear and too happy
>   to permit the presence of trouble.[5]

And to that prayer I would add this last sentence,

> Lord, let me always say
> *Yes* to tomorrow.

2

Say Yes to
GOD'S GIFT OF CHANGE AND GROWTH

If we don't change, we don't grow.
If we don't grow, we are not really living.

Gail Sheehy

If we all just kept on doing exactly what we've done up to now, most people would never change, and people are changing all the time. That's what growth is: doing things you've never done before, sometimes things you once didn't even dream you could.

Mildred Newman and Bernard Berkswitz

When Booth Tarkington, twice a winner of the Pulitzer prize and author of some forty novels, was seventy-five years old, someone asked him whether older people felt old in spirit. His reply was a classic, "I don't know. Why don't you ask someone who is old?"

Born in 1869, just four years after the close of the tragic American Civil War, Mr. Tarkington grew up and grew older during years of expeditious change and expansive growth in American life. And by the time of his death in 1946, he had witnessed revolutionary transformations— in transportation from bulky horse and wagon to sleek aircraft; in communication from Pony Express to radio and the promise of television. In this interval the United States had become densely populated and economically energetic from the rugged shores of the Atlantic Coast on the east to the placid Pacific in the far west. These were exhilarating times in the life of our country—years of radical change and explosive growth. But for a person like Booth Tarkington, change and growth fired his imagination and kept him ever young in spite of the passing years.

In our better and more thoughtful moments, we all know that the comforts and ease of the lifestyle we enjoy now in these closing years of the twentieth century came to us as a result of the restless refusal of our fathers, mothers, grandfathers, and grandmothers to be satisfied with the existing state of affairs. It was the insatiable thirst for the new that forced open the way for change and progress. And it is this same spirit that has unveiled a whole new universe for us as men, women, and machines have penetrated the mysterious outer reaches of limitless space.

Yet there is a strange phenomenon at work within each of us that stubbornly resists change and clings tenaciously to comfortable old ideas and things that remain exactly as they are. With our heads we may accept the idea expressed some twenty-five hundred years ago by Heracleitus of Ephesus who taught that "everything is flowing" and pointed out that a person cannot step twice into the same river because every moment the water changes. But with our hearts we don't want the waters of our lives to be disturbed or changed. For most of us, change for any reason is to be avoided like a cloud of pesky mosquitoes. We resist change with all of the strength we can muster. A friend of ours keeps a little plaque above his desk that reads, "As long as you don't change anything . . . I'm flexible." Sounds strangely familiar, doesn't it?

Our friend Bruce Larson, talented writer and preacher, understood well the human tendency when he wrote,

> Even the most adventuresome of us—those of us who are the least committed to and defensive of the past—still fear change. I've read that people who have been faced with freezing to death in the snow experience a cozy warm feeling that seduces them into inactivity. To stay alive during long exposure to freezing conditions, one has to go against instinctive feelings. To think the way we always have, to act in old patterns is non-threatening and comfortable, but it lulls us toward a frightening death of the soul. To stay alive we must be people on the move, alert to the exciting opportunities of change.[1]

Bruce Larson has expressed a truth that rings true. It is dreadfully easy for most of us to "act in old patterns," to become comfortable with things as they are. Michael Marshall, gifted author and eminent churchman, writes along this line: "There is a warmth and security in the old and the known and the tried ways of life. Part of the power of nostalgia is that it makes no demands upon us to go outside the territory with which we are already familiar."[2]

But if we are to stay alive to the possibilities God has for us, we must each day welcome change—the thinking of new thoughts and the doing of new things—that enables us to grow, develop, and mature in the Christian faith. In fact, "Faith and change are two sides of the same coin. Without faith we cannot change creatively. If we have no goals—no vision—no reason to believe in the future—we cannot create that future."[3]

Frankly, when I'm wrestling with an idea as unsettling as the importance of change in my life, I find it helpful to turn through the pages of my Bible for models among its many heroes and heroines. Again and again in such excursions a moral and spiritual—yet very human—giant moves off the page and onto the center stage of my imagination. His name is Moses.

I won't review here the details of Moses' early life as a child and young adult—years spent as a prince and likely as a scribe in the top levels of sophisticated Egyptian royalty and society. Instead, I'll pick up on the story at that stage of Moses' life when he was somewhere between forty and fifty years of age.

Because of a cataclysmic series of events, Moses had abandoned everything familiar to him and had traveled several hundred miles east and south of his home in Egypt to what is described as "the land of Midian." As were the Hebrews, the Midianites were descendants of Abraham. According to the ancient story, after Sarah died, Abraham married Keturah, and they had six sons—one of whom was named Midian. And evidently by the time of Moses at least some clans of the descendants of Midian lived on the east of the Gulf of Aqaba, one of the branches of the Red Sea.

Because of their common ancestry, Moses undoubtedly felt he would be well received and accepted by the Midianites. And he was. In fact, we're told, according to the Bible story, that Moses was accepted as a member of the household and clan of an important Midianite chieftain by the name of Jethro. And to further seal the relationship, Moses married one of Jethro's daughters, and they had two sons.

Now, while the Midianites were a nomadic people, their culture was quite sophisticated. For example, we know that they were proficient in metal work and that the people of the Kenite clan, to which Jethro belonged, were especially skilled in the metal-working art. They were, in fact, known as the coppersmiths of the desert. All of this is simply to say that Moses with his advanced Egyptian education had every reason to feel at home and comfortable with his adopted Midianite country-people.

And feel at home he did, because he spent many years in Midian. In addition, it is apparent that as the son-in-law of the wealthy and influential Jethro, Moses assumed important and responsible tribal duties and was in charge of at least a sizable portion of his father-in-law's herds of sheep and cattle. It is quite likely, too, that with the passing of the years—just how many we do not know—as Moses managed Jethro's vast herds, he became familiar not only with the immediate environs of Midian but also with at least some portions of the vast Sinai Peninsula a hundred miles or so from Jethro's encampment.

In fact, it was at Mount Horeb (Sinai), probably well over a hundred miles from the comfort and security of his home and Jethro's headquarters that Moses had his encounter with God in the drama of the burning bush, which the Exodus writer reported in vivid detail. The landscape was doubtless familiar to Moses and his men. And it wasn't a particularly unusual sight to see a thorn-bush on fire, because the intense desert heat would often cause a dry and brittle bush to burst into flame. This time something was different. Moses was startled because the bush was not only on fire, but it was not burning up and disintegrating.

You remember the story, I'm sure, but briefly, when Moses' curiosity edged him up to this phenomenon, he immediately learned that he was on sacred ground for out of the bush came the voice of God. And equally frightening, the message was intensely disturbing. After identifying himself and bringing to mind the plight of the Hebrews in Egypt, God said, "I will send you to Pharaoh to bring my people, the Israelites, out of Egypt" (Exod. 3:10).

For Moses this was a most distressing message, and according to the story he put up quite an argument. After all, he had escaped from Egypt many years before as a hunted fugitive. It would be suicide to go back there, and besides, who would believe him? And in addition to all of that, he protested, "I have never been eloquent . . . I am slow of speech and slow of tongue" (Exod. 4:10). But God was persistent, and while going back to Egypt was a terrifying prospect, Moses knew what he had to do.

We have no way of knowing what went on in Moses' mind as he trudged the many miles from the slopes of Mount Horeb north and around the narrow branch of the Red Sea and then south to Jethro's encampment. Surely wild and bizarre thoughts must have raced through his mind. And we just have to believe that during those long and lonely hours, he was reminded again and again of the comfort and security of his pleasant life with his family and friends; it was ridiculous to leave everything he had come to know and love behind! And yet, according to the story, when Moses arrived back at the tent of his father-in-law, he said, "Please let me go back to my kindred in Egypt" (Exod. 4:18).

Next, as the adventure unfolds, we find Moses on his way back to Egypt to fulfill his destiny. It had to be an agonizing time in many ways for him as he confronted the uncertainty of the future. As the Bible drama plays out, we catch the scenes of Moses standing up against Egypt's Pharaoh and ultimately, with God's help, leading the Israelites out of their slavery across the arid wilderness to the very mountain where he had had his burning-bush encounter with God. No longer tongue-tied and fearful, he was now a political and military leader of his people. And it was at Sinai that he assumed the role of spiritual leader of Israel and received the living words of the Ten Commandments from God on the mountain summit above the clouds.

Yes, Moses must have had to struggle bitterly with the agony of change and the risk it involved. In the process, he grew to become the man who justly merited the accolade of the Deuteronomy writer, "Never since has there arisen a prophet in Israel like Moses, whom the LORD knew face to face" (Deut. 34:10).

As we reflect on the Moses saga and the model he has given us for saying *Yes* to change and growth, we become increasingly aware of the fact that this is both a rewarding and at the same time painful experience because it frequently means separating ourselves from the known and the familiar. Yet it can be a rewarding time as we respond to God's guidance.

One further thought before we leave the Moses story. While the chronology cannot be exact, Moses' dramatic change likely took place when he was well past the allotted three score and ten. This is an important thought because it underscores the fact that we never grow too old to change.

Saying *Yes* to change and growth means that at every stage and age we are living beyond the usual boundaries of life. In his book *Learn to Grow Old*, Dr. Paul Tournier reminds us of these important words of General Douglas MacArthur, who in 1945 at the age of sixty-five said, "You don't grow old from living a particular number of years; you get old because you have deserted your ideals. Years wrinkle your skin; renouncing your ideals wrinkles your soul. Worry, doubt, fear, and despair are the enemies which slowly bring us down to the ground and turn us to dust before we die."[4]

Wrinkled souls filled with worry, doubt, fear, and despair—such a description goes against everything God intends for us as people created in the image of God. Instead, as children of the King, each new day is meant to be lived in a spirit of anticipation and excitement. Most certainly, a gloom and doom attitude is anti-Christian—it goes against everything Jesus modeled for us in his life, death, and resurrection.

In the last few years I have become increasingly aware that our late twentieth century world is plagued by a dull and lackluster sameness. Cities, towns, neighborhoods, houses, fenced yards, and, yes, people, all take on a sort of flat, dull sameness, almost as if they were stamped out by a cosmic cookie cutter. It seems that many people suffer from an overdose of humdrum. Every day is the same—work, eat, watch television, and sleep. Can it be that we have become prisoners of the way things are?

Even many Christians seem to have become victims of the dullness virus, and we've become dyspeptic and even belligerent when confronted with new ideas, with new expressions, and by people who obviously do not wear our particular label. We resist having our little boats rocked by any wave of change. Our values and attitudes have become calcified, and we refuse to let our dull and comfortable routines be challenged or disturbed in any way.

A generation ago Dorothy Sayers, an exceptionally talented British Christian and writer, recognized the truth of this when she wrote, "Somehow or other, and with the best of intentions, we have shown the world the typical Christian in the likeness of a crashing bore—and this in the name of One who assuredly never bored a soul in those thirty-three years during which he passed through the world like a flame."[5]

Indeed the Gospel writers give us a picture of a Jesus who was attractive to the crowds of ordinary people who dogged his footsteps and made him a welcome guest at parties and celebrations. It is interesting, isn't it, that his first recorded public appearance after his baptism was at a wedding celebration in the little community of Cana in Galilee. No, there wasn't anything dull and boring about this Jesus whose mission was to make all things new and to plant the seeds of change and growth.

And there was nothing dull and commonplace about the people who appear on the pages of our New Testament drama. In fact, early Christianity was a vibrant and explosive force that worked exciting change throughout all of the Mediterranean world during the first century. Life for them was full of novelty and spontaneity. There was an attractive effervescence about them that shouted *Yes* to life. They were not *trying* to change; it just happened, and their joy and vitality was instantly contagious.

One of my twentieth-century spiritual heroines is Mrs. Charles E. Cowman, the author and compiler of several best-selling devotional books that have nourished my soul for many years. On one occasion she wrote, "Somewhere near the snowy summit of the Alps there is an inscription that marks the last resting place of an Alpine guide. Just three short words tell the story, 'He died climbing.' We often hear it said that 'so and so is growing old.' But we don't *grow* old. We only *get* old when we cease to grow and climb."

It is interesting, though, that as we grow and climb, the panorama of our lives changes constantly. The terrain doesn't necessarily become easier or more level, but as our perspective changes and matures, we are better able to confront life's challenges with the same kind of zest that characterized those early New Testament Christians. Somewhere among his prolific writings Dr. B. F. Skinner, insightful interpreter of human nature, observed, "Older people who see themselves as doing useful and interesting things fare better in every way than ones who merely take it easy."

Another gifted writer, Evelyn Underhill, underlines this same idea, "To be spiritually alive means to be growing and changing; not to settle down among a series of systemized beliefs and duties, but to endure and go on enduring the strains, conflicts and difficulties incident to development."[6]

"Be spiritually alive"—yes, that is the goal for each of us. And, yes, this calls for us to be open to change as we move through the various stages of life. From change comes new growth and the doing of new things. In fact, I have slowly come to see that this is the keynote in our Christian pilgrimage. I like the way an old friend has translated what the apostle Paul had to say about newness when he wrote these words to his friends in the bustling city of

Corinth, "From this time on, then, let us look at others not with our limited human insight. Although we have perceived Christ humanly, let us no longer look at him that way." Because, "if any person has been joined with Christ . . . *he or she is a new person*; the old way of looking at life has passed away, and from this new perspective *everything has become fresh and new*."[7]

I have often been challenged by an exchange between the gifted poet and writer of past years, Henry Wadsworth Longfellow, and a friend and admirer of his. While the two were visiting one day, the friend noted Longfellow's cotton white hair, which was in vivid contrast to his ruddy complexion and animated spirit. Knowing that the poet was well along in years, his friend asked how he was able to remain so alive and vigorous and to write so beautifully.

In reply Longfellow pointed to an apple tree nearby that was loaded with brilliantly colored blossoms. "That apple tree," he said, "is very old, but I never saw prettier blossoms upon it than those it now bears. The tree grows a little new wood each year, and I suppose it is out of the new wood that these blossoms come. Like the apple tree I try to grow a little new wood each year."

"A little new wood each year"—that is to be our goal as followers of the New Way and as citizens of Jesus' New Society. This is the recipe for colorful change and growth. And as I reflect on my life—from the rural cotton town of Italy, Texas, to Hollywood, and in later years to the California high desert community of Victorville where we established the Roy Rogers–Dale Evans Museum—I am amazed at the "new wood." There have been times of effervescent joy and hours of searing heartbreak. Yet like the kaleidoscope I loved as a child, with each movement the scene changes and the sparkling combinations of color are more beautiful.

Little by little I have come to see that it is movement and change that bring spice and drama into our lives at whatever age and stage we are, especially as we move into mid-life and beyond. In reality, mid-life and the later mature years are times "for discovery, not stagnation." These are times "ripe for fresh beginnings. . . . If approached with good humor, flexibility, and an openness to change, the middle years and beyond can be the best half of life."[8] Yes, it is in the doing of new things in a planned and calculated way that we find the inspiration to cast off our prefabricated prejudices and assembly-line attitudes.

Samuel H. Miller was a warm and devoted Christian of a generation or two ago. He acquired a world of wisdom as the pastor of Old Cambridge Baptist Church and Dean of Harvard Divinity School, but his little book entitled *The Life of the Soul* may well be his greatest legacy. In it Dr. Miller issues this challenge, "The only way in which we can grow into something better than we are now is to do things we're not strictly able to do. We will have to subject ourselves to certain disciplines, the practice of exercises which we will not do well at first, and will take a great deal of failing before we accomplish the satisfactions of a skillful soul."[9]

It was this spirit that motivated another Old Testament hero of mine. Undoubtedly, everything in the Sumerian city of Ur of the Chaldeans was familiar and quite predictable to Abraham. But the biblical narrative tells us that he and his family left Ur and traveled north to Haran, a stopping point on the way to Canaan, the final destination. And next we read that after staying in Haran for a time the Lord said to Abraham, "Go from your country and your kindred and your father's house to the land that I will show you" (Gen. 12:1). It must have been a frightening thing for seventy-five-year-old Abraham to move out from the familiar and the known to the unfamiliar and the unknown, but he did. And for Abraham, life began at seventy-five because by faith Abraham obeyed God as he set out, not knowing where he was going. Imagine! That is *change* in capital letters.

Here is the secret. It is *by faith* that we can say *Yes* to all of tomorrow's change and growth. And as we move out in faith, we may not know exactly where we are going any more than Abraham did, but the same Lord who guided him each plodding step to his Promised Land will guide us. It is true we will not know the how, where, and when of God's leading, and at times the route and the timing may seem puzzling, but we can take comfort in the confidence that wherever we are, Christ has been there ahead of us.

You remember that when Joshua and the people of Israel were poised on the east bank of the Jordan River at flood stage opposite the city of Jericho they had no set of detailed instructions and no road map. All they had was God's promise, "I will be with you," and the priests carrying the ark of the covenant were told to move forward and step into the water. And it wasn't until they got their feet wet that a miracle happened—the way across was clear and they could proceed toward their tomorrow.

3

Say Yes to
GOD'S GIFT OF JOY AND LAUGHTER

Joy to the world! the Lord is come;
Let earth receive her King;
Let every heart prepare Him room,
And heaven and nature sing.

Joy to the world! the Savior reigns;
Let men their songs employ;
While fields and floods, rocks, hills and plains,
Repeat the sounding joy.

Isaac Watts

In a letter from Parson John to Miriam Gray come these pearls of wisdom:

Many of the religious people that I know, when they talk of religion, have a bedside manner and walk about in felt slippers. And if they speak of God they always tidy themselves first. But you go in and out of all the rooms in God's house as though you were quite at home. You open the doors without knocking, and you hum on the stairs, and it isn't always hymns either. My aunt thinks you are not quite reverent; but, then, she can keep felt slippers on her mind without any trouble.[1]

Yes, that is a quaint communication out of the old English past, and yet it is somehow descriptive of the somber point of view prevalent among many Christians today. But this "felt slippers on the mind" attitude doesn't match up with the exuberant joy and laughter that is God's gift to everyone who follows him and attempts to walk in Christ's footsteps.

Dr. Norman Vincent Peale in one of his sermons tells about the importance of joy and laughter as portrayed in a *Reader's Digest* article written by Bob Hope, the colorful and ageless radio and television personality. The setting for Bob Hope's story was 1948; General Dwight D. Eisenhower had just been appointed to the presidency of Columbia University. A great convocation of faculty and thousands of students came together to honor and greet the new president.

When General Eisenhower walked onto the platform, he confronted a super-serious audience that was at expectant attention in anticipation of a sedate call to serious study and sober living. However, the general displayed his world-famous grin and said, "Have fun! I mean it. The day that goes by without your having some fun—the day you don't enjoy life—is not only unnecessary but unchristian!"

General Eisenhower was, as usual, right on target. Over and over again the Bible spells out a clear message that God intends for us, his people, to be joyful and happy and, yes, to show it with hearty laughter. This doesn't mean, of course, that we will not experience difficult and trying times and endure both pain and sorrow. The ancient wisdom writer understood the ebb and flow of human emotions when he wrote that there would be "a time to weep" and "a time for mourning," but he counterbalanced that by saying that we would also have "a time to laugh" and "a time for dancing" (Eccles. 3:4 NEB).

Although the psalmist was well acquainted with the rigors and dangers of rustic life in the Judean hills and in the merciless climate and terrain of the Negev, he could still sing, "You will show me the way which leads to life: with You there is abundant joy; enjoyable things result continually from Your generosity."[2] And another wisdom writer quipped that when the people of God are happy "they smile" (Prov. 15:13 TEV).

Philo, the Alexandrian Jewish philosopher who lived in the time of Jesus, is quoted as saying, "God is the creator of laughter that is good." But laughter and joy are not only God's creation, they are his gift to people in all of time, and as such, they, along with all of God's creation, are "very good." Martin Buber, the erudite Jewish theologian and philosopher commented on one occasion, "The heartbeat of life is holy joy."

The power and influence of joy and laughter are vividly illustrated in the lives of two extremely gifted and creative men. The first is Franz Joseph Haydn, whose genius sparked brightest in the mid-to-late 1700s and very early 1800s. He is credited with over one hundred symphonies and a vast array of other musical creations of varying styles. But Haydn's legacy also included a vigorous and intense devotion to God, as evidenced in part by his comment, "When I think of God, my heart is so full of joy that the notes leap and dance as they leave my pen; and since God has given me a cheerful heart, I serve him with a cheerful spirit." And out of this cheerful and joy-filled spirit came the magnificent oratorio *The Creation* and other compositions that have enriched the worship of Christians to this day.

The second gifted person who comes to mind is very much front and center on today's scene. Novelist James A. Michener was born into a Quaker household. He has this to say in his memoirs, "I was raised in an atmosphere of love, responsibility, and service, but what I remember most is the constant laughter in our home."[3] From *Tales of the South Pacific* in 1947 (a Pulitzer Prize winner) to *Mexico* in late 1992, James Michener's creative output of books has brought joy, happiness, and laughter to millions of people around the world—a glowing tribute to the constant laughter that dominated his Quaker boyhood home and has added spice and creative genius to all of his life and experiences.

This same spirit comes through clearly in a comment made by Dr. Samuel M. Shoemaker, that giant of a preacher who served major churches in New York and Pittsburgh a generation ago and whose writings have enriched the lives of thousands of people. For him, "The surest mark of a Christian is not faith, or even love, but joy." In truth, Sam Shoemaker had the faith, love, and devotion that contributed to the establishment of Alcoholics Anonymous and the Pittsburgh Experiment—both lifesaving institutions that have given new life and hope to thousands of hurting people. But it was his joyful and cheerful spirit that gave vigor to his ministry and attracted people to him. Indeed, it was his joy, faith, and love that doubtless prompted this comment by Dr. Billy Graham, "I doubt that any man in our generation has made a greater impact for God on the Christian world than did Samuel Shoemaker—a giant among men."[4]

Unfortunately, all too often skeptical people engaged in the struggle to find some kind of sense and order in our complex and complicated world are confronted by a somber and combative form of Christianity. Instead of infectious laughter bubbling up out of a full life enlivened by the Spirit of God, we Christians tend to sometimes model an exclusive and at times even an angry faith— one that erects towering barriers before anyone who does not see, understand, and express things our particular way.

Somehow, without intending to, our priorities have become confused. We have lost contact with the spirit of the angelic announcement to the awestruck and terrified Bethlehem shepherds, whose peaceful evening had been interrupted and disturbed by the intrusion of bright lights and angels in the night sky. According to the Gospel writer who described the scene, an angel in an effort to ease their terror said to them, "Do not be afraid; for see— I am bringing you good news of *great joy for all people*: to you is born this day in the city of David a Savior, who is the Messiah, the Lord" (Luke 2:10–11, italics mine). The coming of Jesus was a time for joy, laughter, and singing. His coming split history; the world and its people in all of time would never be the same again.

Somehow, too, we have become strangers to this Jesus of "good news and great joy" who with the passage of time became the Jesus who was attractive to the crowds and enjoyed a good time. Over and over again the Gospel writers picture Jesus being present at dinner parties and social functions. There are a number of references to Jesus attending dinner parties and intimate gatherings at the home of Mary, Martha, and Lazarus in Bethany. And we cannot help being a little amused over the grumbling of the self-righteous Pharisees because Jesus was at ease with tax collectors and sinners (Luke 15:1–2). He must have put them at ease by his caring and convivial spirit. While it is true that none of the Gospel writers speaks of Jesus' laughter, it is not stretching things to assume that people wanted to be around him because of his happy manner. After all, no one enjoys being around a grump, and harbingers of gloom aren't the least bit attractive and don't make good party and dinner company.

Jesus set the stage for this attitude toward all of life at the very earliest stages of his public ministry. The setting is what we know as the Sermon on the Mount. Matthew pictures Jesus speaking to vast crowds of people from a hillside, probably overlooking the Sea of Galilee. Dr. J. B. Phillips has given us a delightful translation of these beautiful words:

> How happy are the humble-minded. . . .
> How happy are those who know what sorrow
>   means. . . .
> Happy are those who claim nothing. . . .
> Happy are those who are hungry and thirsty for
>   goodness. . . .
> Happy are the merciful. . . .
> Happy are the utterly sincere. . . .
> Happy are those who make peace. . . .
> Happy are those who have suffered persecution for
>   cause of goodness. . . .
>
> [Matt. 5:3–10 *Phillips*]

Perhaps we are more familiar with the King James Version and Revised Standard Version, which employ the word *blessed* where Dr. Phillips and other modern translators prefer the word *happy*. Jesus, of course, spoke in Aramaic, the common language of his day. We don't really have an English equivalent for the word Jesus used, but in effect he was saying, "Oh, how very blessed," or, "Oh, how effervescently happy." Pictured in the Beatitudes is a bubbling joyfulness and happiness of the kind usually expressed by exuberant laughter.

The late Dr. William Barclay, the erudite Scottish Bible scholar from Glasgow whose stated mission in life was to interpret biblical truth in the language of "the common man," says of these Beatitudes that they "are not the pious hopes of what shall be; they are not glowing, but nebulous prophecies of some future bliss; they are congratulations on what is. The blessedness which belongs to the Christian is not a blessedness which is postponed to some future world of glory; it is a blessedness which exists here and now. It is not something into which the Christian *will enter*; it is something into which he *has entered*."[5]

In other words, this gift from God is an unrestrained and glowing joy and happiness that floods through and over the life of the Christian in spite of the difficulties and heartaches that are inevitable in our human pilgrimage. These are not fanciful flashes of some future happiness but concrete assurances for the down-to-earth world in which we are now living.

Then toward the end of Jesus' ministry the Gospel writer moves us into some intimate scenes as he talks with his disciples and close friends. At one point he says, "I have said these things to you so that my joy may be in you, and that your joy may be complete" (John 15:11).

And between the Beatitudes and these last words of Jesus we have volumes of teachings and parables that give us glimpses into a very real and human Jesus whose humor seeps through and illuminates his profound teaching. Jesus, in fact, was a master storyteller whose comparisons and descriptions were often flavored with the subtlest forms of humor—irony and exaggeration. The Gospel writers of Matthew, Mark, and Luke especially seemed to catch the earthy humor in Jesus' teachings. And while laughter is not spoken of, many of the scenes and settings give strong hints of a smile and even laughter.

Over the years I've been enriched and challenged in reading those New Testament books credited to the apostle Paul. I've always had the notion that he was a very intense and no-nonsense kind of a person, not much given to seeing or expressing the lighter and more humorous and happy side of things. Yet I have to believe there was a happy and joyous side to this great apostle—possibly even to the point of laughter now and then. In writing to his close Christian friends in the Roman colony of Philippi, he gave them and us a hint of his feelings when he wrote, "I want you to be happy, always happy in the Lord; I repeat, what I want is your happiness" (Phil. 4:4 JB).

As we reflect on the Bible drama and on the vast array of Christian saints who have moved back and forth on the stage of history, we are no doubt easily convinced that God has indeed given to us and to his people in all of time his gift of joy, laughter, and happiness. It was said of the early Christians that they could be easily identified because of their joyful and loving manner. We have to believe that they did not go around with long faces and worried creases in their foreheads. Rather, they had accepted God's gift of joy and laughter and had nurtured that gift until it could be readily seen in every part of their lives.

God has given us so much, and the challenge for each of us as believers in Jesus Christ is to respond with contagious joy. Author Harold Kushner very wisely put his finger on an extremely important point when he wrote, "In the Talmud, the collective wisdom of the rabbis of the first five centuries, it is written, 'In the world to come, each of us will be called to account for all the good things God put on earth which we refused to enjoy.'"[6]

The inspired writers of our Bible insisted that the world and all of God's magnificent creation is ours to enjoy. And for the Christian it is a big and wonderful world as described so often by the writers of the Psalms—a world in which the fingerprints of God are seen in all that he has made.

One of the most winsome and electric television personalities of the past generation was Archbishop Fulton J. Sheen. He beautifully captured the idea that the Christian way of life was intended to be one of unrestrained joy and laughter. His quick wit and penchant for humorous and delightful stories coupled with a winsome and contagious smile made him one of the most convincing voices for God that has ever shown up on television. In his autobiography Bishop Sheen made this sagacious comment, "The amount of humor that anyone gets out of the world is the size of the world in which he lives."[7]

Any expression of Christianity that fails to illuminate God's gift of joy and laughter is incomplete and inadequate. While the joy-filled Christian is aware of all of the hurt, suffering, and injustice present in our world, he or she is unquestionably convinced that God is still in charge—ultimately, all's right in God's world!

4

Say Yes to
GOD'S GIFT OF PRAYER

The paradox of prayer is that we have to learn
how to pray while we can only receive it as a gift.

Henri J. M. Nouwen

Our Father, who has set a restlessness in our
hearts and made us all seekers after that which
we can never fully find . . . keep us at tasks too
hard for us, that we may be driven to Thee for
strength.

A prayer Eleanor Roosevelt
carried in her purse

The year was 1952. The setting was Rice University
stadium in Houston, Texas. The event was the citywide
Billy Graham Crusade. The audience was made up of
forty-five thousand attentive and eager listeners.

I was sitting on the platform with tears in my eyes. Roy was at the podium, speaking. It was Roy's first witness to a crowd of this size.

"Dale worked with God to bring me something I had longed for all of my life—peace. Materially speaking, for years I had nothing. Then for years I had much. But I soon learned that having too much is worse than having too little. Nothing ever seemed quite right. I was restless, confused, unsatisfied. But then I learned that the power of prayer and the feeling of spiritual blessedness and the love of Jesus have no price tags."

The stadium was locked in a dead silence. It seemed that all of the forty-five thousand people were holding their breath for what would come next. Roy went on to describe the strength he gained through daily prayer and reflective Bible reading. Then he closed his witness by denying the published rumors that he was thinking of leaving show business and becoming an evangelist. "If I was going to be an evangelist," he smiled, "I guess I'd have to do it on horseback, because being a cowboy is all I know." And as Roy's smile gave way to a wide boyish grin, the crowd melted and broke out with thunderous applause.

Yes, God's gift of prayer has been a powerful sustaining force in our home for many years—through difficult times as well as in good times. And this we know for sure, prayer—agonizing prayer—saw both of us through the two years that we cared for our little Robin, our Down's syndrome baby, our *Angel Unawares.* When she left us to be with her heavenly Father, it was prayer that kept us steady. It was prayer—ours and those of our friends—that saw us through the tragic deaths of our daughter Debbie on the church bus and our son Sandy in Germany.

More recently, Roy and I have had reason to rely with
deep feelings of gratitude on the gift of prayer as each of
us has weathered heart attacks and surgery—mine as
recently as the spring of 1992. In all of this we've been
reminded over and over again of the definition of prayer
given us by one of our Bible teachers. She told us that
prayer should be: first, praise of God; second, thanks-
giving for his love and guidance; and, third, petition for
ourselves and our needs. And the final word was, "You
can trust him implicitly for the answer."

How true! Yet there have been those days—yes, weeks
and even months—when it seemed that God was strangely
silent to my heartaches and hurts. But slowly I've come
to understand just a little bit the truth behind these
thoughts of Henry Ward Beecher, the powerful nineteenth-century preacher, who wrote in his little book entitled *Aids to Prayer*, "Think not that God's silence is cold-
ness or indifference! When Christ stood by the dead, the
silence of tears interpreted his sympathy more wonder-
fully than even that voice which afterwards called back the
footsteps of the brother [Lazarus], and planted them in
life again. When birds are on the nest, preparing to bring
forth life, they never sing."

An unindentified writer made this intriguing comment,
"There is no music in a rest, but there is the making of
music in it." In the melody of our lives' experiences we
often come to those times of silence and "rests." It is
important in such moments not to feel that the life-
melody is over but to look expectantly for the next movement to begin. God is still the divine Conductor.

In our humanness we fall victim so often to the notion
that God should act on our schedule and timetable and
in ways that we can readily understand. There is an ever-

present danger that we may come to see prayer as a form of heavenly room service. We tend to lose sight of the truth that the purpose of prayer is not to change God or to activate him. Rather the purpose of prayer is to change us. I like the way author Søren Kierkegaard expressed this idea, "Prayer does not change God, but changes him who prays."

Author Henri Nouwen enriches our understanding of prayer as he writes that when "prayer makes us reach out to God, not on our own but on his terms, then prayer pulls us away from self-preoccupations, encourages us to leave familiar ground, and challenges us to enter into a new world which cannot be contained within the narrow boundaries of our mind and heart." Then Dr. Nouwen adds, "Prayer, therefore, is a great adventure because the God with whom we enter into a new relationship is greater than we are and defies all calculations and predictions."[1]

Along this same line of thought is a comment credited to the late William Temple, the ninety-eighth Archbishop of Canterbury, "When I say my prayers, I find that coincidences begin to happen." On the other hand, it is important that we strive for an understanding of prayer that avoids it misuse. Dr. James Houston cautions against this in his perceptive book entitled *The Transforming Friendship*, "It is alarmingly easy for prayer to become a kind of magical device which we use to get our own way."[2]

This leads us in our Christian pilgrimage to not only say *Yes* to God's gift of prayer but to also pose the same request that Jesus' disciples put to him one day. Luke speaks of the incident in these words, "Once, in a certain place, Jesus was at prayer. When he ceased, one of his disciples said, 'Lord, teach us to pray'" (Luke 11:1 NEB).

Jesus' response to this request was simple and uncomplicated but very much to the point:

> Father, may your name be honoured—may your kingdom come! Give us each day the bread we need, and forgive us our sins, for we forgive anyone who owes anything to us; and keep us clear of temptation.
>
> [Luke 11:2–4 *Phillips*]

This has become known as "the Lord's Prayer"—certainly the supreme model for us of the gift of prayer. While the Luke wording of Jesus' response to his disciples is considerably shorter than the one found in the Gospel of Matthew (see Matt. 6:9–13), it gives us in a nutshell everything essential to our coming to an understanding of how we are to use God's gift of prayer and what we are to pray for.

Space prohibits me from making an exhaustive commentary on the Lord's Prayer, but in a few words I want to express a little of what it has come to mean to me. First, Jesus prays, "Father." This was the traditional opening for any Jewish prayer. However, in this instance Jesus used a most untraditional Aramaic word for *Father—Abba*. This is the word a child would have used in speaking to a human father. *Father* as Jesus used it here gives us a sense of intimacy, respect, and reverence that shifts prayer from a ritual to a profound personal and intimate experience and relationship—quite the opposite to a flippant or casual approach.

For Jesus, the Father was not a vague, faraway entity but an intimate and nearby Father—one who cares deeply about everything that concerns us. The apostle Paul expressed it this way for those first-century Christians who were struggling with the idea of this kind of God:

> To prove that you are sons, God has sent into our hearts
> the Spirit of his Son, crying "Abba! Father!" You are
> therefore no longer a slave but a son, and if a son, then
> also by God's own act an heir.
>
> [Gal. 4:6 NEB]

Next in the model prayer Jesus said, "May your name be honoured" or "hallowed be your name." This heavenly Father of ours is also the Creator-God who spoke the universe into existence and is to be revered. In the words of Isaiah the prophet, he is the Holy One. Over the centuries Christian believers have struggled long and hard for a human understanding of God, and in that struggle the temptation to bring him down to our size often rears its ugly head.

Human experience makes it clear that we will never understand God in this life, but we are to revere all that we do understand him to be. Saint Augustine put it very succinctly when he said, "If you have understood, then what you have understood is not God."

We get a deeper understanding of what is happening in this prayer Jesus taught his disciples as we realize that the reference to God's name goes far beyond the way we use the word. To the Jews *name* referred to a person's total character. To pray, "may your name be honoured," means "far more than knowing that God's name is Jehovah. It means that those who know the whole character and mind and heart of God will gladly put their trust in him."[3] And in praying "May your kingdom come," we are asking that God's will may become a reality to Christian believers now and in all of the future.

The writer of the Matthew version of the prayer adds this sentence, "Thy will be done in earth, as it is in heaven" (Matt. 6:10 KJV). It seems to me that this is the

central petition of the Lord's Prayer even as it is to be
central in all of our praying. Only then can we move on
to the remaining petitions of the prayer.

A close look at how prayer is treated in the Book of
Acts gives us the pattern the early Christians followed
under the leadership and teaching of the apostles—their
prayers were always for God's will to be done, even as
they prayed for others. For them, and for us, prayer is
intended to be an intimate part of all of life—not something reserved to be used when we're in trouble or at
eleven o'clock on Sunday morning.

As I mentioned earlier, Dr. Samuel Shoemaker in his
books and sermons had a most perceptive way of con-
veying truth. On one occasion he said, "Prayer is not calling in the fire department; prayer is seeking to live so that
the house does not get on fire. Prayer is not the 'last
resort,' it is the first thought in every situation . . . Prayer
is communion between two 'people' who increasingly
know each other. And one of these 'people' is very decid-
edly a Senior Partner in the relationship."[4]

So far, in the Lord's Prayer our attention has been
focused on God:

> Our Father in heaven,
>   hallowed be your name.
>   Your kingdom come.
>   Your will be done,
>   on earth as it is in heaven.
>   [Matt. 6:9–10]

Now the focus shifts to us and our needs:

> Give us this day our daily bread.
> And forgive us our debts,

as we also have forgiven our debtors.
And do not bring us to the time of trial,
but rescue us from the evil one.

[Matt. 6:11–13]

First, Jesus directed our thoughts to God and his will for everyone. Now comes the acknowledgment that this same God is concerned about and equal to our needs here and now; he forgives our sins and wipes out our debts; and, finally, we can look to the future in confidence, knowing that the Father will support us in our times of testing and trial.

Behind all of Jesus' teaching is the truth that the Father is a God of love who cares intimately for each one of us. St. Teresa of Avila, a devout sixteenth-century Spanish Christian, captured the true meaning of prayer when she said, "Prayer is not a matter of thinking a great deal but of loving a great deal." In writing to Christians everywhere and in all of time, the writer of the Book of Jude counseled his readers with these words, "But you, my friends, must fortify yourselves in your most sacred faith. Continue to pray in the power of the Holy Spirit. *Keep yourselves in the love of God*" (Jude 1:20–21 NEB, italics mine).

Reflecting on God's gift of prayer to people like us is an awesome experience. In a sermon entitled "The World's Greatest Power: PRAYER" Dr. Norman Vincent Peale asks the question, "What is the greatest power in the universe?" In response he adds, "Is it the enormous force of the hurricane or the tornado, or the tidal wave, or the earthquake, or the exploding volcano?" He then defines this power in these electric phrases, "I believe that it is the mechanism by which man on earth establishes a connection that provides the flow of power between the

mighty Creator and himself, between the great God who
scattered the stars in the infinite night sky and the crea-
ture made in his own image: man. The flow of power
between the Creator and man is the world's greatest
power. And it is released and transmitted by means of a
mechanism known as prayer."[5] But it is a power that calls
for action on our part if it is to be effective.

One of the greatest and most endearing preachers of
the past generation was Dr. Paul S. Rees. He had the
knack of packing profound truth into a few words, "If we
are willing to take hours on end to learn to play the piano,
or operate a computer, or fly an airplane, it is sheer non-
sense for us to imagine that we can learn the high art of
getting guidance through communion with the Lord
without being willing to set aside time for it. It is no accident that the Bible speaks of prayer as a form of waiting
on God."[6]

In the midst of our busy and hectic lives a first step to
this "waiting on God" may involve putting into practice
an idea suggested by Dr. Frank Laubach. Picking up on
the pray-without-ceasing principle as expressed by the
apostle Paul, Dr. Frank suggested instant or quick prayers
right in the middle of the hustle and bustle of life: A sentence prayer while sitting in the doctor's waiting room,
"Lord, bless the doctor and give him wisdom." Or a
prayer for Jane after dialing her number and waiting for
an answer, "Bless Jane, Lord, as she takes on her respon-
sibilities in her new job." Or while waiting for a bus or a
taxi or an airplane, "Oh God, guide the hand of the dri-
ver (pilot) and give us a safe trip." Or while sitting prayer-
fully in your pew at church waiting for the service to begin,
"Father, speak to me this morning and help me to be
open to you and everyone around me." Waiting at the sig-

nal for the red light to turn to green . . . while standing
in the grocery checkout line . . . while walking four laps
in the mall or while walking the dog in the early morning hours—all of these daily routines offer the opportunity for prayer fragments that can enrich our own lives
and the lives of the people we are praying for.

In the early centuries of the Christian church the
Desert Fathers, quite likely in the vicinity of Mount Sinai,
put together a very simple ten-word prayer that has
become known as "the Jesus Prayer": "Lord Jesus Christ,
Son of God, have mercy on me." Throughout the centuries both clergy and lay people have seen in these few
words the summation of the Christian faith, and it is used
widely by people who pray in all parts of the world as a
means of grace and a sustainer of the faith.

An unknown writer left us this gem:

> Prayer is so simple;
> It is like quietly opening a door and
>   slipping into the very presence of
>   God.
> There in the stillness
> To listen to his voice,
>   perhaps to petition
>   Or only to listen.
> It matters not,
>   Just to be there, in his presence . . .
> Is prayer.

Another unknown writer left behind these incisive
reflections on the Lord's Prayer.

> I cannot pray *our*,
>   if my faith has no room for others and their needs.

I cannot pray *Father*,
> if I do not demonstrate this relationship to God in
> my daily living.

I cannot pray *who art in heaven*,
> if all my interests and pursuits are in earthly things.

I cannot pray *hallowed be Thy name*,
> if I'm not striving with God's help to be holy.

I cannot pray *Thy kingdom come*,
> if I am unwilling or resentful of having it in my life.

I cannot pray *on earth as it is in heaven*,
> unless I am truly ready to give myself to God's
> service here and now.

I cannot pray *give us this day our daily bread*,
> without expending honest effort for it,
> or if I would withold from my neighbor the bread
> that I receive.

I cannot pray *forgive us our trespasses as we forgive those
> who trespass against us*,
> if I continue to harbor a grudge against anyone.

I cannot pray *lead us not into temptation*,
> if I deliberately choose to remain in a situation
> where I am likely to be tempted.

I cannot pray *deliver us from evil*,
> if I am not prepared to fight and resist evil.

I cannot pray *Thine is the kingdom*,
> if I am unwilling to obey the king.

I cannot pray *Thine is the power and the glory*,
> if I'm seeking power for myself and my own glory
> first.

I cannot pray *forever and ever*,
> if I am too anxious about each day's affairs.

I cannot pray *Amen*,
> unless I can honestly say,
>> "Cost what it may, this is my prayer."

Our pastor, the Rev. William Hanson, prayed this prayer, which I have taken as my own, "Lord, we confess that we cling to a safe and comfortable faith. We are not looking for challenges, and we do not like to take risks. Forgive us for taming your gospel and reshaping your teachings to our liking. Forgive us, Lord, and help us to break free from the false security of our own comfort to the true security of faith. Change us in such a way that we may become willing to risk our hearts and lives in following and serving you. Amen."

5

SAY YES TO GOD'S GIFT OF WONDER

If you accept this Gospel
and become Christ's man,
you will stumble upon wonder upon wonder,
and every wonder true.

Brendan to King Brude

The ancient Judean poet-sheepherder was divinely inspired one night to write and reflect on his overwhelming awareness of all that was going on around him. These were his thoughts, and we can be eternally grateful that his words have been preserved for us.

Oh God, how full of wonder and splendor you are!
I see the reflections of your beauty and hear
    the sounds of your majesty wherever I turn.
Even the babbling of babes and the laughter of
    children spell out your name in
    indefinable syllables.

> When I gaze into star-studded skies and attempt
>   to comprehend the vast distances,
> I contemplate in utter amazement my
>   Creator's concern for me.
> I am dumbfounded that you should care personally
>   about me.
> And yet You have made me in Your image.
> You have called me Your son.
> You have ordained me as Your priest and chosen
>   me to be Your servant.
> You have assigned to me the fantastic responsibility
>   of carrying on Your
>   creative activity.
> O God, how full of wonder and splendor
>   You are![1]

In this present-day translation of the awe-inspiring psalm we catch the poet's almost inexpressible amazement at the wonder of God's world. At the same time, there is the awareness that in some mysterious way in creating us in his image he has bequeathed to us the gift of wonder. We sense his utter amazement over everything that comes from God.

Like the psalmist on a star-studded night, Robert Louis Stevenson, the gifted nineteenth-century novelist and essayist, captured this sense of wonder one night in Calistoga at the north end of Calilfornia's Napa Valley. His magnificently descriptive prose reveals the depth of his feelings.

> I have never seen such a night. . . . The sky itself was of a ruddy, powerful, nameless, changing color, dark and glossy like a serpent's back. The stars by innumerable millions stuck boldly forth like lamps. The Milky Way

was bright like a moonlit cloud; half heaven seemed Milky Way. The greater luminaries each more clearly than a winter's moon. Their light was dyed in every sort of color—red, like fire; blue, like steel; green, like the tracks of sunset; and so sharply did each stand forth in its own lustre that there was no appearance of that flat, star-spangled arch we know so well in pictures, but all the hollow of heaven was one chaos of contesting luminaries—a hurly-burly of stars.

While Robert Louis Stevenson made no direct reference in this descriptive piece to God as the author of the wonders he was seeing, we know that in some way he was in tune with the Creator of it all, for in another piece he said, "There is nothing but God's grace. We walk upon it; we breathe it; we live and die by it; it makes the nails and axles of the Universe."

People throughout all of human history—from the beginning, whenever that was, to the present—have in their thoughtful moments been moved in reverence by the wonders of God's world. In contemplating those wonders, many have seen them as testimonies of his fatherly and caring involvement in everything that concerns us.

Yes, there are those who have been unwilling to acknowledge God in the wonders of our universe and others who claim to believe that all of this, including life itself, is the result of some kind of cosmic accident. Such ideas, though, just do not square with our deepest feelings. It has been suggested that the chance of life originating from some sort of cosmic accident would be comparable to a leather-bound copy of an unabridged dictionary appearing full-blown after an explosion in a book manufacturing plant.

Far more believable and satisfying is this assertion of
the psalmist,

By the word of the LORD the heavens were made,
and all their host by the breath of his mouth.
He gathered the waters of the sea as in a bottle;
he put the deeps in storehouses.
Let all the earth fear the LORD;
let all the inhabitants of the world stand in awe of him.
For he spoke, and it came to be;
he commanded and it stood firm.
[Ps. 33:6–9]

In a moment of inspiration the ancient wisdom writer
agreed with the psalmist when he wrote,

The LORD created the earth by his wisdom;
by his knowledge he set the sky in place
His wisdom caused the rivers to flow
and the clouds to give rain to the earth.
[Prov. 3:19–20 TEV]

But perhaps the most amazing of God's wonders is his
gift of wonder to us, as we saw earlier when, in a flash of
insight, the psalmist reminded us that we are made in
God's image and are his chosen sons and daughters. Having said that, the psalmist added, "You have assigned to
me [us] the fantastic responsibility of carrying on Your
creative activity."[2]

What an incredible wonder and assignment! What a
glorious legacy we have as God's special people. It is hard
to believe, and yet as we view the wonders of just the last
few years, we can only say, "Thank you, Lord, for the gift
of wonder." For in our lifetime we have come to take the

Among the large number who had become believers *there was complete agreement of heart and soul.* Not one of them claimed any of his possessions as his own but everything was common property. The apostles continued to give their witness to the resurrection of the Lord Jesus with great force, and a wonderful spirit of generosity pervaded the whole fellowship.

[Acts 4:32–33 *Phillips,* italics mine]

The drama and wonder of the resurrection miracle from those early days of Christianity until today is beautifully expressed by author Frederick Buechner. In *Telling the Truth* he says it is "the outlandishness of God who does impossible things with impossible people."[6]

It is easy for us to identify with the "impossible people." But how grateful we are for the "outlandishness" of God, who through Jesus Christ has given us the fantastic experience of carrying on his creative activity.

Wonder of wonders!

6

Say Yes to
GOD'S GIFT OF FRIENDSHIP

> The friend who can be silent with us in a
> moment of despair or confusion, who can stay
> with us in an hour of grief and bereavement,
> who can tolerate not-knowing, not-curing, not-
> healing, and face with us the reality of our
> powerlessness, that is the friend who cares.
>
> Bernie S. Segal

Being a friend and having friends are, without question, among the greatest gifts of God's magnificent creation schemes—awesome gifts to each of us from a caring heavenly Father.

It is easy, though, in the frantic rush of our busy twenty-
four-hour days to become so self-preoccupied that we fail
to be a friend. Yet as we progress through the various
stages of our lives, we are conscious in our more thoughtful and honest moments of just how much we need each

other for the enrichment of our own life experiences and personal growth.

In the early 1940s, through an intriguing combination of circumstances, a Hollywood agent named Art Rush became a part of my life. Following a stint as a singer on CBS radio station WBBM in Chicago, I had signed a one-year contract with Twentieth Century Fox motion picture studios in Hollywood under the guidance of an agent named Joe Rivken. During that year I got just two bit parts, and all the signs seemed to indicate that my contract would not be renewed. The studio moguls had decided that I looked too much like their current top star, Betty Grable, to be built up and featured.

At that same time I confess that I felt like a fish out of water—I understood radio, but motion pictures were something else. So, I asked Joe Rivken to recommend a Hollywood agent who was at home in the radio world. I remember Joe's response as if it were yesterday, "There is just one man in all of Hollywood that I would trust you with. And his name is Art Rush."

I contacted Art Rush immediately, and arrangements were made for me to sing for him and his wife, Mary Jo. Following the audition, which went off well, Art said, "I think I know just the spot for you. There's an opening for a female vocalist on the 'Chase and Sanborn Hour'"—the show that featured Edgar Bergen and Charlie McCarthy, Don Ameche, and orchestra leader Ray Noble.

Art arranged for the audition, and I sang for Edgar Bergen, Ray Noble, and the show's producer Tony Sanford. I felt pretty sure I had the job when that crazy puppet Charlie McCarthy gave me a shrill whistle through his wooden mouth. I smiled, Edgar Bergen smiled, and

Art Rush smiled. A few days later I signed a contract, and for the next thirty-nine weeks I appeared on the show as the featured female vocalist. It was a choice spot—prime time, five o'clock Sunday afternoon. This was just the break I needed on one of the most popular shows of that time.

During those weeks Art Rush and I were together a great deal. In our conversations I learned that Art was a devout Christian. As a young man he had gone to Bethany College with the idea of becoming a minister, but he soon felt this was not his calling. However, Art's commitment to God remained the most important thing in his life. He said to me one time, "Dale, God is the Director of my life." This wasn't hard to believe, because his actions and soft-spoken demeanor squared with his words.

Again and again in our conversations Art brought up the name of a singing cowboy client of his, Roy Rogers. Art was very proud of Roy, who at that time was number one in western pictures. We had not met yet, but a little later I was singing at Edwards Air Force Base in California's Mojave Desert and was scheduled to appear with Roy Rogers and the Sons of the Pioneers. It was then Art introduced me to his singing cowboy protégé. No sky rockets went off, and no bells rang in my head. Roy Rogers seemed to me at that time to be just a shy, mannerly cowboy with striking good looks and a nice singing voice—nothing more, nothing less.

In the meantime I'd had a call from a person at Republic Studios who had heard me sing, and I was asked to go out there and audition for them. That audition produced a one-year contract, and two weeks later I was in rehearsal for a movie entitled, "Swing Your Partner." During that year I did seven more films and must have toured every army base in the southwestern United States.

After my Republic contract was renewed, Mr. Yates, the head of Republic Studios, called me one day and said, "Our Roy Rogers westerns have been doing very well, and I think they would go over even better if we had a female lead who was a singer and had a radio following. I think you are what we are looking for." Then he added, "Rehearsals for 'The Cowboy and the Senorita' will begin next week. You're the senorita." The year was 1944.

B-Westerns weren't exactly what I had in mind for a career, but I went along with Mr. Yates's directive, and before that year was over I had made three more pictures with Roy. Finally, after a series of events, I left the studio and went my own way. In 1947, however, while I was doing an engagement in Atlantic City, I looked out into the audience and saw Art Rush and Roy Rogers. We talked after the show, and it wasn't long before I was back at Republic working with Roy.

On New Year's Eve of 1947 Roy and I were married at the Flying-L Ranch near Davis, Oklahoma, with Art Rush as Roy's best man and Mary Jo Rush as my matron of honor. For the next fifty-some years Art Rush represented both Roy and me. He was the closest and best friend either of us ever had. He was with us in our successes, and he shared those agonizing moments at the deaths of three of our children.

Roy and I have many poignant memories of time spent with Art, but etched into our minds forever is a picture of him the night before he died. He couldn't speak, but Art looked at us as we stood at the foot of his bed, and with a light in his eyes he formed these words with his lips, "I love you."

Art Rush truly epitomized the "true friend" described by one of the Bible's wisdom writers,

> Some friends play at friendship
> but a true friend sticks closer
> than one's nearest kin.
> [Prov. 18:24]

In another place this same writer said, "A friend loves at all times" (Prov. 17:17). The very wise and insightful writer of the apocryphal Book of Ecclesiasticus further described what Art Rush means to us,

> A faithful friend is a secure shelter;
> whoever finds one has found a treasure.
> A faithful friend is beyond price;
> his worth is more than money can buy.
> A faithful friend is an elixir of life,
> found only by those who fear the Lord.
> The man [person] who fears the Lord keeps his
>   friendships in repair,
> for he treats his neighbour as himself.
> [Ecclus. 6:14–17 NEB]

Keeping our friendships in repair is a salient ingredient of our relationships. It has been said that we have a custodial responsibility to maintain our friendships.

Noted Christian historian and author Dr. Martin E. Marty has written a marvelous book on friendship. In it he speaks of friendship as being "a gift of God." He writes, "To be a friend may mean to be the most important person in the world to someone else over a period of years."[1] Most certainly, friendship involves giving ourselves unreservedly to others; it involves accepting others unconditionally and being *with* them—really being with them in their failures as well as in their triumphs.

As I have continued to reflect on the enormous impact Art Rush had on our lives through his gift of friendship, I have been reminded of a quality of his that I think made him the kind of a person he was. He *really* listened to us— he didn't just *hear* us, he *listened* to us. I've come to understand that we hear with our ears, but we listen with our hearts! Art always listened to us with his heart.

The Bible's wisdom writers have a great deal to say, overtly and covertly, about the importance of listening in our relationships. This idea has its greatest expression in the Bible story of King Solomon, who achieved greatness because of his wisdom. When Solomon was crowned king upon the death of this father David, we're told that God appeared to him in a dream or vision and asked him, "What shall I give you?" Solomon responded with a lengthy answer, but the heart of what he asked for was simply this, "Give thy servant . . . a heart with skill to listen, so that he may govern thy people justly and distinguish good from evil" (1 Kings 3:9 NEB). The New Revised Standard Version of this same verse reads, "Give your servant therefore an understanding mind." Both readings are quite correct with the original Hebrew— *listening* and an *understanding mind* are one and the same.

The ancient wise men of Israel well understood the importance of listening, and time hasn't changed that. We all have a desperate need to listen to our friends and to be listened to.

Paul Tillich, noted theologian of a past generation wrote somewhere, "The first duty of love is to listen." Another very wise person is reported to have said, "Listening is a key to *knowing* and *understanding*." It seems to me that is what friendship is all about—it is knowing and understanding another person and being known and understood by another person.

Throughout the Bible we encounter a parade of friendships that serve as models for us. Perhaps the classic and most profoundly moving story is found in the Old Testament book of First Samuel. In chapters 18, 19, and 20 the writer features the relationship between Jonathan, King Saul's son, and David, the shepherd-boy giant-killer from Bethlehem. The biblical writer tells us that "Saul's son Jonathan was deeply attracted to David and came to love him as much as he loved himself. Jonathan swore eternal friendship with David because of his deep affection for him" (1 Sam. 18:1, 3 TEV). As proof that this was not just a surface friendship, Prince Jonathan sealed the relationship publicly, at considerable risk to himself, by giving David his royal robe and his prized weapons—his sword, bow, and belt—all emblems of his royal position as the king's son and a prince in Israel.

Two things leap out at me in this Jonathan and David friendship story. First, the ancient and very wise writer makes the point that Jonathan loved David "as his own soul" (NRSV)—as he loved himself. With Jonathan, as with each of us, the capacity for friendship emerged from healthy self-esteem and self-acceptance. This idea was first suggested by the Leviticus writer centuries before when he recorded God's words to Moses, "You shall love your neighbor *as yourself*" (Lev. 19:18, italics mine). Jonathan seemed to understand that well and applied it to his own life.

The second thing that stands out sharply is that David accepted Jonathan's gift of friendship and the symbols of that gift. From that time on, in spite of setbacks and reverses, David moved steadily toward becoming Israel's greatest king and earned a place in God's Hall of Fame as listed in Hebrews 11. I have to believe that his early friendship with Jonathan was a vital chapter in David's story.

Dr. Leslie Weatherhead wrote in one of his books, "If I were to say in one sentence what Christianity is, I think I should say that it was the acceptance of Christ's friendship." Then he added, "Christianity began in friendship."[2]

How true! Early in the story of Jesus we understand how important friends and friendship are to him, and from him we learn an invaluable lesson. We see in Jesus' actions and selections that he was inclusive. By contrast, in exercising our own gift of friendship, we are prone more often than not to select for friends only those people who see, believe, and express things the way we do. Most of the time our friends are *our* kind of people who are comfortable with our particular patterns and prejudices. All too often we insist that *our* friends think and speak only with our social and spiritual vocabulary.

When Jesus selected the twelve men to be his special friends and followers at the very beginning of his public life, he was amazingly inclusive. They were ordinary, everyday people—most of them were rugged and weather-beaten fishermen. Early on we learn that James and John were hot-tempered, self-serving, and instinctively ambitious. Peter was volatile and impetuous, and more often than not suffered from foot-in-mouth disease. Matthew was a customs and tax collector—a profession notorious for greed and crooked dealing, despised by the Jews and classed with murderers and robbers. In fact, tax collectors were excluded from the judicial system and excommunicated from public worship—not even their offerings were acceptable. Simon was a zealot—a political fanatic—as was James the Younger. And it is thought likely that Judas Iscariot was also a member of the explosive zealot group. Philip was apparently more respectable than the rest but was an avowed pessimist.

The original Twelve were a diverse and unlikely lot. Given the chance, you and I would not have picked them to be friends or members of our church committees. Yet, all but one turned out to be effective and devoted leaders in the Jesus movement. In fact, someone has wisely said that the group of rugged individualistic men, some devout women, and assorted folks from the fringes of society became so transformed because of their friendship with Jesus that they turned the first-century world upside down. We ask: What made the difference? It was their intimate relationship with Christ and devotion to each other as friends. These people gave us a relationship model and a mission for spiritual living that will serve us well as we move into the twenty-first century.

Very briefly, I want to refer to another friendship model in the Bible drama. At an early stage the lead character in this friendship saga was a man known to us as Barnabas, a feature actor who appears in the very heart of the Book of Acts. Actually, his name was Joseph, and although he was a Jew, he was a native of Cyprus, an island in the northeastern corner of the Mediterranean Sea. Joseph was an early convert to Christianity and had become a member of the church in Jerusalem. It was there he was given the surname of Barnabas—a word that in Hebrew means "son of encouragement" (Acts 4:36).

Barnabas moved to center stage in the Acts story with the arrival in Jerusalem of Saul of Tarsus, who we also know as Paul, the Greek version of his name. We know that after Paul's confrontation with Christ on the Damascus road, he went into seclusion for an extended period of time. Later he traveled to Jerusalem, undoubtedly to identify with and be accepted by the Christians there, but they rejected his overtures out of fear. After all, they remembered well this same Saul, a rigid Pharisee, who had not too long before persecuted any believer in Jesus that he could track down—no Christian had been safe from his bitter and ruthless attacks. There was just no way they were able to believe his story and accept him. But Barnabas befriended Paul, believed his story, and vouched for him so that he was finally accepted into the Christian community. After that, though, we read that Paul left Jerusalem and returned to his home city of Tarsus.

In the meantime, Christianity was spreading rapidly out from Palestine, and a strong community of believers was formed in the Syrian city of Antioch. Barnabas was sent by the Jerusalem church to shepherd these new Christians, but soon he needed more help and support. So Barnabas left Antioch and traveled north to Tarsus in search of his friend Paul. After an extensive hunt Barnabas located Paul, whom he persuaded to accompany him back to Antioch, and they worked together in this church where believers in the Way were first called Christians.

During this time together Barnabas probably exerted a profound influence on Paul's thinking and his understanding of the Christian faith and message. It is obvious that their friendship ripened, because we soon find the two of them working and traveling together on a missionary trip to the island of Cyprus and then on to Asia Minor under the sponsorship of the Antioch Christians. While this was a relatively short trip, they were able to establish a number of new churches. It was a successful trip, even though young John Mark, who had started out with them, turned back and returned home before they had gone too far. Apparently John Mark's leaving was very irksome to Paul.

Barnabas and Paul hadn't been home long after that first trip before they decided to start out again and visit the churches they had established earlier and then extend their efforts to communities they had not visited before. This time, however, the two friends had a strong disagreement. Barnabas wanted to give his young cousin John Mark a second chance and take him with them, but Paul strongly disagreed because he had deserted them on the first trip. To Paul, John Mark was a quitter and did not deserve a second chance. Because of this difference of opinion, the two men decided to separate. Paul took another companion on the trip with him, and Barnabas, still the friendly mentor and encourager, took John Mark and went off in another direction.

We have only the bare bones of the story, but I don't think it stretches our imaginations too much to picture Barnabas as seeing that Paul was now well established in the faith and didn't need him as much as he had before. On the other hand, young John Mark sorely needed the friendship and guidance of his older cousin at this crisis time of his life.

Once again, Barnabas—the "son of encouragement"—was a mentor and friend to one who needed his support and guidance. Even as his friendship with Saul of Tarsus (Paul) had produced a vibrant and energetic Christian witness and an encourager of Christians, new and established, now Barnabas shifted his influence to another promising young man. A future isolated reference and early tradition places John Mark in positions of church leadership and credits him with being the author of what we know as the Gospel of Mark. Additional tradition credits John Mark with being the first to preach the Good News of Jesus Christ in Egypt and of being the founder of the large and influential Christian community in Alexandria.

What a marvelous heritage of friendship this man Barnabas has passed along to us. For we are all called to be sons and daughters of encouragement to people along the way. Someone has wisely said that we cannot be Christians in a vacuum. Most certainly, we need each other to be all that God wants us to be. Author Scott Peck, in his best-selling book entitled *The Road Less Traveled*, states that love is "the will to extend one's self for the purpose of nurturing one's own or another's spiritual growth."[3] That is a true expression of the gift of friendship.

Several years ago a man named Allen Emory, longtime associate of Billy Graham, wrote a delightful book entitled *Turtle on a Fencepost*.[4] According to Allen Emory, many years ago a person would at times come across an unusual sight while walking down a country lane in New England—a turtle would be perched right on top of a fencepost. One thing you could know for sure was that there was just no way that turtle could have gotten up there by himself. Someone had to stoop down, pick up the turtle, and set him on his fencepost perch.

The point of the illustration and the book was simply this: We are all turtles on the fenceposts of our lives. Over the years friends and mentors have had confidence in us and have given us the lift and encouragement necessary to be where we are. At the same time, each of us is called upon to exercise our gift of friendship and lift up and encourage others so they can be all that God wants them to be.

In reflecting on the Barnabas story and the turtle-on-the-fencepost parable, my thoughts have floated back over the years to a couple of people whose gift of friendship has been a powerful and sustaining force to me. The first was just a little girl when I first knew her. It was shortly after Roy and I were married, and we were living in Hollywood. Our two children, Cheryl and Linda, had become friends with two little neighborhood girls.

Judy, one of the little girls, became almost like a daughter to me. Her family didn't attend church, but she became interested and began attending Fountain Avenue Baptist Church with us, and after a time she accepted Christ as her Savior. Over the many years since that time, Judy has remained a fast friend and has stood by me during times of heartbreak and tragedy. For example, when our Debbie was killed in the 1964 bus accident and Roy was confined to a hospital because of a spinal fusion, it was Judy who spent the long and painful night with me. When I had my heart attack on May 10, 1992, she visited me regularly in Loma Linda Medical Center, and I knew she was praying constantly for me.

Another close friend, Marguerite Hamilton, shared my heartbreak in 1950 when our Robin came into the world as a Down's syndrome baby. I had met Marguerite and her wonderful daughter Nancy just shortly before Robin was born. Nancy's hands and feet were badly deformed, and she was one of the sweetest children I have ever known. All through Robin's two years in this world, Marguerite and Nancy were a great consolation to me. Although both Robin and Nancy have gone on to be with their heavenly Father, Marguerite has remained a close and supportive friend over these many years.

Through God's marvelous provision of the gift of friendship, I have been made stronger over the years by Roy and my family and by a great host of friends. They have given me strength for today and hope for all of the tomorrows to come.

Dorothy Baird, another staunch Christian friend, beautifully expressed my deepest feelings in her poem "Forever Friends."

> Friends who know us and yet love us
>   are often hard to find.
> They share in our sadness;
> They help bring us gladness
>   and continue to be so kind.
> Whether separated by miles,
>   or daily sharing smiles,
> We remain true friends of the heart.
> We meet, hug, and talk.
> Share a meal, take a walk
>   as though we've never been apart.
> Our faults, they forgive us;
> Our problems they share with us.
> They're generous with compassion and love.
> Not just friends in the sunshine,
>   but friends through a lifetime;
> They're sent from the Lord above.
> Thank God for true friends
>   whose love never ends. . . .
> Those special, forever friends.

7

Say Yes to GOD'S GIFT OF RISK AND DIFFICULTY

Inevitably, living the Christian life is a risky
adventure—one pregnant with difficulties. But
for the Christian, Jesus reminds us, "In the
world you have trouble [risk and difficulties].
But take heart! I have overcome the world."

Olaf M. Norlie

In George Bernard Shaw's play *Saint Joan* there is a
powerful statement about the risk and danger in our faith
and Christian pilgrimage. Before sentence was passed on
Joan of Arc, Bishop Cauchin said to her, "My child, you
are in love with religion." In response Joan asked, "I never
thought of that; is there any harm in it?" To which the
bishop answered, "No, my child. There is no harm in it.
But there is danger."

Today, we are inclined to think that the risk and danger
of being a Christian dates back to the fifteenth-century

world of Joan of Arc. Yet in 1980 the civilized world was shocked at the death of four missionaries in El Salvador. As I write this in late 1992, the newspapers headline the tragic story of five Catholic nuns from Illinois who were killed in a suburb of Monrovia, Liberia.

Most of us, though, are not risking our lives as Christians. Nevertheless, if we are faithful to our commitment to Christ, there are other subtle forms of risk that threaten us. True, we think of risk, difficulties, and dangers as being threats, but as I've thought about God's provisions for our growth and spiritual health, I have come to believe that risk is one of God's gifts—as painful as it may be at times.

In the recent past there has been an epidemic of criticism directed toward members of the United States Congress and accompanied by a kind of raw cynicism. It is true, of course, that there are those who have flagrantly abused their power and privileges, betraying the trust their constituents have placed in them. This sort of thing has been going on since the days of the ancient city-states in the Middle East.

However, since the forming of our government in the late eighteenth century, our Congress and national leadership have been made up of men and women of principle who were—and are—willing to risk their political reputations by adhering to their convictions. Many of these have been and are committed Christians.

Among them is an old friend of ours, the Honorable Mark O. Hatfield, the senior senator from the state of Oregon. Several years ago Senator Hatfield wrote a book titled *Between a Rock and a Hard Place*. In it he recounted numerous incidents in which his Christian convictions clashed with what would seem to be politically expedient. For him, these were times of painful risk.

Of the several stories Senator Hatfield told, one especially piqued my interest. The time was early 1973. Senator John Stennis of Mississippi asked Senator Hatfield to speak briefly to the National Presidential Prayer Breakfast in Washington, D.C., on behalf of the Senate Prayer Group. At the time discussions and feelings about the American action in Vietnam were at a fever pitch, and it was widely known that Mark Hatfield, out of strong Christian conviction, was personally opposed to the government policy at the time.

After wrestling with whether or not to accept Senator Stennis's invitation and after consulting with friends and associates from whom he received conflicting advice, Senator Hatfield decided to honor the invitation of his friend. In doing so he was reminded that among the three thousand guests at the prayer breakfast would be the president and other national leaders. "My intention," he wrote, "was to say some word which would be relevant to them, and faithful to my own convictions; to give a faithful witness to truth and to my Lord."

Senator Hatfield arrived at the meeting that morning and took his seat at the head table. "I began to sense the tension growing inside me," he wrote. "My long-time friend Billy Graham was seated next to me on my left; President Nixon was on my right. Cabinet officers and other members of Congress were all nearby. I could not help but think, am I going to make a fool of myself before all these friends and associates? It was that feeling we all know which bids us to go along with the crowd, or not to risk doing something that may displease people whose friendship we deeply value. These thoughts and feelings flashed through me."

The full text of Senator Hatfield's remarks offered a thoughtful and respectful statement of his feelings. A short yet moving excerpt merits our attention. The Senator said, "We sit here today as the wealthy and powerful. But let us not forget that those who follow Christ will more often find themselves not with the comfortable majorities, but with the miserable minorities. Today our prayers must begin with repentance. Individually, we must ask forgiveness for the exile of love from our hearts. And corporately as a people, we must turn in repentance from the sin that scarred our national soul." He closed with these words, "We must continually be transformed by Jesus Christ and take his commands seriously. Let us be Christ's messengers of reconciliation and peace, giving our lives over to the power of his love. Then we can soothe the wounds of war, and renew the face of the earth and all mankind."

During Senator Hatfield's remarks, he caught the hostile looks of certain leadership people. In the days that followed it became clear that even though he had made no direct mention of the Vietnam war or the president that there were those who interpreted the incident "as a direct confrontation with the President."[1]

Throughout Mark Hatfield's long political career—first as a representative in the Oregon State Legislature, then as a state senator, a two-term governor of Oregon, and a United States senator since 1966—he has placed his reputation and career in jeopardy as often as necessary in obedience to what he believed was God's will for his life. The response to the risks involved is the ongoing respect of both those who have agreed with him and those who have disagreed.

Roy and I have usually been good risk takers. Two incidents in particular stand out in my mind. The setting for the first incident was in New York City. Just three weeks after our little Robin died, we were scheduled for an appearance in Madison Square Garden. The show had been booked two years before, and we felt we should keep the date even though our feelings were raw from the loss of our loved one.

In planning for the show Roy decided that he wanted to sing "Peace in the Valley," because it was the Lord's peace and sustaining grace that was enabling us to go through with the commitment. The song was—and is—a great favorite of Roy's, and he wanted its witness to be felt by everyone in attendance.

After we arrived at the Garden, Roy and The Sons of the Pioneers worked up a beautiful arrangement of "Peace in the Valley." Roy then made arrangements with the light crew to darken the Garden at a certain place in the song and throw a lighted cross on the turf by means of special lighting.

At the dress rehearsal everything went off beautifully. When Roy reached that place in the song, "the lion will lay down with the lamb," the house went dark and the lighted cross was brilliant against the dark turf. It was most effective. Immediately after the rehearsal, however, the Garden management called us to the front office and said, "You cannot show that cross in this show. You'll have to take it out."

Roy looked the manager right in the eye and said, "No, that cross has a special meaning for us at this time. The cross stays in." In response the manager said, "Impossible. You cannot do it." And with that Roy said, "Then get yourself another cowboy. Dale and I are going back to California." The Garden management hadn't expected this, so they finally gave in and agreed the lighted cross effect could stay in.

Our first performance was an afternoon matinee, and the balcony was full of teenagers from parochial schools on Long Island. When Roy reached that climax in "Peace in the Valley" and the cross appeared on the floor of the darkened Garden, those young people jumped to their feet and cheered with a deafening roar of approval. That convinced the Garden management, and the cross stayed in for all of the remaining performances. The risk Roy took paid off. When we risk for God, he *will* honor our efforts.

The second incident occurred when we were invited by the Billy Graham Association to participate in the first London Crusade. Since we had not been there before, we planned to arrive ahead of time and do a tour of several of the major cities in England, Scotland, and Ireland. The British producer arranged for these appearances because at that time the British Roy Rogers fan club was the largest one in the world.

For the Glasgow appearance we decided that after our regular program we would do a little salute to God and country. I mentioned how important the Bible was to us and that we were in this part of the world to participate in the Billy Graham Crusade, and I urged the people to go down and hear him. We then closed out the evening by singing "God Save the Queen" and "How Great Thou Art."

When word got to the producer about our little addition to the secular show, he called Art Rush on the telephone and said, "We didn't hire those people to preach. We hired them to entertain. Tell Dale Evans to quit talking about God and Billy Graham." I told Art everything would stay just as it was, and we then went ahead in spite of the producer's complaints.

Before our scheduled Belfast appearance, the producer called Art and told him to warn me that those Irish Catholics would probably throw garbage at me if I boosted the Graham meetings. I went ahead anyway, and at the conclusion of the program we were given a standing ovation—the only time that happened on the entire tour. Then as I was about to leave, one of the ushers came up and told me that someone wanted to see me in the wings.

My visitor was a lovely Irish monk who identified himself as the chaplain of the Abbey Players. Then he said, "I want to ask you a very personal question; I hope you will answer it for me. What kind of a man is Billy Graham?" I said, "Sir, he is the most utterly consecrated Christian that I have ever had the privilege of knowing." With that, he extended his hand, took mine, and said, "I knew it." Once again, the risk had produced positive results—God is always faithful!

As I've thought about these risk stories, I have been reminded of that parade of biblical people who took formidable risks. One of them is an unnamed woman; the writers of both the Gospel of Mark and the Gospel of Luke tell her story. In setting the scene the Gospel writers picture Jesus walking down the street in the middle of a crushing crowd.

In that crowd was a desperate woman who had suffered with a hemorrhage for twelve years. This was apparently a common illness at that time, and Jewish lore specified at least eleven cures for the debilitating ailment—some were obviously quack remedies, while others had a reasonable chance of success. We are told, though, that noth-

ing had helped this woman in spite of the fact that doctor
bills had wiped her out financially.

When she saw Jesus in the crowd, she knew that he was
the one who had become famous in Galilee as a healer.
So she decided on the spur of the moment to take a risk—
she would slip up behind him unobtrusively and touch
the fringe on the bottom of his robe with the hope that
she would be healed. Such a brazen action was an out-
rageous intrusion because her illness, according to Jewish law, made her ceremonially unclean. This simply
meant that anything or anyone she touched would also
be unclean. Then, too, there was the risk of discovery,
but she decided to take the chance. It isn't hard to picture the scene as she slipped up behind Jesus, bent over
when no one was looking, and gingerly touched the fringe
of his robe.

At that moment, though, her world fell apart, for Jesus
whirled around and asked, "Who touched my clothes?"
In understandable amazement Jesus' disciples said, "You
see the crowd pressing in on you; how can you say, 'Who
touched me?'" Then in embarrassment and fear the
woman identified herself—she was the guilty person.
With this admission, Jesus assured her that she was
healed, and he told her that her faith had made her well.
She had met Jesus, and it was worth the risk. (See Mark
5:25–34; Luke 8:43–48.)

Among the many risk takers in the Bible drama is
another very unlikely character—Nicodemus. He appears
in just two scenes, but both are highly significant. First,
we encounter Nicodemus, a proud Pharisee and a dis-
tinguished member of the Jewish Council, talking with
Jesus under cover of darkness. Even under those circumstances, he was risking a great deal if he was caught

talking to this subversive teacher. The super-religious Pharisees and the Temple hierarchy labeled Jesus a heretic and a disturber of the peace. To be sympathetic with him was to invite trouble and harassment.

Nicodemus decided, as did the woman in the crowd, that the encounter was worth the risk. For it was to Nicodemus that Jesus said, "No one can see the kingdom of God without being born from above." And it was to Nicodemus that Jesus spoke these immortal words, "For God so loved the world that he gave his only Son, so that everyone who believes in him may not perish but may have eternal life" (John 3:3, 16).

The second scene with Nicodemus finds him taking an enormous risk as he joins Joseph from the village of Arimathea in removing Jesus from the cross and burying his body in the Garden Tomb. (See John 19:39–42.) We can gather from this bold action that for this once proud and self-righteous Pharisee the risk had been worth it, for it is obvious that he had indeed been "born from above" and was no longer skittish about being recognized as a follower of the Galilean.

While we're looking at risk takers in our New Testament drama, we don't dare overlook Zacchaeus. The scene for this delightful story was the city of Jericho, a bustling center on an important east-west highway. It was a rich community of balsam groves and date palms that were owned largely by King Herod and the royal family.

Zacchaeus was probably the chief tax collector in Jericho and was a man of considerable wealth. Apparently he had heard that the Galilean preacher and healer would be passing through town on his way to Jerusalem. Curiosity got the best of Zacchaeus, and since he was a short man and was unable to see over the taller folks who lined the street, he risked looking foolish, climbed up a tree, and shinnied out onto a limb that hung over the crowded street. Certain that he wouldn't be observed, he felt comfortable in spite of his awkward perch.

Wonder of wonders, when Jesus reached a spot just below Zacchaeus, he looked up and said, "Zacchaeus, hurry and come down; for I must stay at your house today." With that, Zacchaeus risked the ire of the religious authorities and did exactly what Jesus had requested. In fact, we're told that Zacchaeus was "happy to welcome him." The risk of looking foolish and then entertaining an unpopular traveling preacher paid off because of his remarkable conversion and moral turnaround. (See Luke 19:1–10.)

In this marvelous story Zacchaeus got the full treatment. That's the way God works! Author C. S. Lewis understood this well when he gave us this delightful bit of wisdom,

> When I was a child I often had a toothache, and I knew that if I went to my mother she would give me something which would deaden the pain for that night and let me go to sleep. But I did not go to my mother—at least, until the pain became very bad. And the reason I did not go was this. I did not doubt she would give me the aspirin; but I knew she would also do something else. I knew she would take me to the dentist the next morning. I could not get what I wanted out of her without getting something more, which I did not want. I wanted immediate relief from pain; but I could not get it without having my teeth set permanently right. And I knew those dentists; I knew they started fiddling about with all sorts of other teeth which had not yet begun to ache.[2]

To the serious person there is no partial conversion—no quick fix.

As St. Paul discovered, living the Christian life is a risky business. As long as he was a respectable, synagogue-going Pharisee who obeyed the religious rules and fulfilled the rituals, he lived a risk-free and comfortable life. However, after meeting the risen Jesus on the Damascus road and after being converted under the guidance of Ananias, his life from then on was full of risk and danger. Yet it is apparent that it was worth the risk and danger for the great apostle. He testified to this in a letter to his "son" Timothy not long before his death,

> I have fought the good fight, I have finished the race, I have kept the faith. From now on there is reserved for me the crown of righteousness, which the Lord, the righteous judge will give me.
>
> [2 Tim. 4:7–8]

Let's face it, though. In spite of what we have learned from such biblical models as the sick woman on the crowded street, Nicodemus, Zacchaeus, and Paul we all strive desperately to lead comfortable, secure, successful, and risk-free lives. We often strive for the understanding of our friends and associates at the expense of taking an unpopular stand that is dictated by our spiritual and moral principles.

There is something more here, however, that seems important. I think we often avoid taking risks because of the fear of failure. Somehow everything about our culture puts a premium on success and a stigma on the possibility of failure, but this doesn't square with the way things work. Recently, I saw a program featuring Mark Goodson, the creator of many top television game shows.

The interviewer asked Mr. Goodson what percentage of the shows he had written were successful. After a thoughtful silence he said, "One out of five." That means four out of five wouldn't be classed as successful in today's television world. Isn't it amazing then that Mr. Goodson is great because of the one out of five that are successful?

In 1992 Tom Seaver, pitcher for the New York Mets, was elected to Baseball's Hall of Fame with a win-loss lifetime record of 311–205. He won 311 games, but he lost 205 games—he failed 205 times, but being willing to risk that, Tom Seaver had the enviable record of 311 games won. Yes, the risk of failure is always there, but in the game of life we are to concentrate on the positives.

One thing for sure—in our passion to avoid rocking life's boat and to avoid risk, we miss the stretching experiences of life as God intended it to be when he created us in his image. I just don't believe it was God's intention for us to play it safe and take it easy. Paul Tournier set the mood when he wrote, "My wish for everyone is that they will be jolted from time to time by life, and that they will be faced with the need to make new departures," and he urges us to avoid becoming "prisoners of duty."[3] In his wonder-filled book entitled *The Meaning of Persons*, Dr. Tournier wrote about the adventure of living a rich and meaningful life, "It means accepting risks: 'nothing ventured, nothing won,' says the proverb. We think that by being cautious we are protecting life, whereas we are slowly smothering it. Our Lord's words come to mind: 'Whoever will save his life shall lose it' (Mark 8:35)."[4]

Dr. Alan Jones records a question and answer exchange between the eloquent Jewish writer Elie Wiesel and a questioner: "He was once asked about the difficulty of believing in God after the experience of the Holocaust—

is belief possible after Auschwitz? Wiesel responded that if it was hard to live in a world without faith in God, it was even harder to live a life of faith. If you want difficulties, choose to live with God."[5]

As Christians we need to be reminded daily that the symbol of Christianity is not a padded rocking chair, nor a dollar sign in the bank book, nor a paid-up health care plan. No, the symbol of Christianity that is recognized around the world is the cross. Remember, the miracle of Easter morning was made possible by the cross.

Most certainly, even a sketchy look at the life of Jesus when he was here on earth reflects a life of risk from the human point of view. From the beginning of his life of public service at Cana in Galilee to his crucifixion and death on Golgotha outside the walls of Jerusalem, Jesus risked his life in the fulfillment of his earthly destiny. All of this made possible the Easter miracle of his resurrection. Then after his return to the Father, his disciples and early followers risked their lives again and again in making the Good News available to people everywhere.

Author John Knox expressed it well when he wrote, "The primitive Christian community was not a memorial society with its eyes fastened on a departing master; it was a dynamic community created around a living and present Lord."[6]

Those first- and second-century Christians modeled for us in an unforgettable way the risk involved in living the life of faith. It wasn't easy, and their very lives were frequently on the line, but they said *Yes* to God's gift of risk and moved on to change the world. For them and for us, the game of life involves moving boldly to accept this gift from the Lord as we make our way each hour of the day.

In his *The Miracle of Easter,* Floyd Thatcher wrote, "An unidentified war correspondent in a rare moment of inspiration wrote these moving lines:

> Some men die by shrapnel,
> Some go down in flames.
> But most men perish inch by inch
> Who play at little games.

The Miracle of Easter points to a lifestyle not of mediocrity and littleness but to one of 'big games.' It involves risk and venturing and change as we move toward the wholeness which God has designed for each of us."[7]

8

GOD'S GIFT OF FAITH

The life of faith is not a life of mounting up with wings, but a life of walking and not fainting. . . . Faith never knows where it is being led, but it loves and knows the one who is leading.

Oswald Chambers

Faith can only originate in the soul of man by the gift of God.

Marcus L. Loane

Early morning in our high desert home near Victorville, California, is my special time of being alone with the Lord. There's a clean aroma in the invigorating morning air, and the birds nesting in our trees sing their approval of the bright new morning. As I look out across the vastness of the rolling hills dotted with yucca and other desert

95

will not let me go even if my very own family should turn against me. He will sustain me and keep me on course through the dangers and pitfalls of this life. It is possible to know and experience God's love in this uncertain, tumultuous existence. Take courage, step out in faith, scorning consequences. Let God have his way with you.[1]

This twenty-seventh Psalm was a powerful faith document for David Jacobsen, director of the American University of Beirut's Medical Center, during his seventeen torturous months as a hostage held by the Hizballah, the dreaded archfundamentalist Muslim terrorists. Mr. Jacobsen's ordeal began on May 28, 1985, when he was abducted at gunpoint on a Beirut street, forced into a van, clubbed by his kidnapper's gun butt, and spirited away.

Mr. Jacobsen's months of captivity are a horror story that is almost unbelievable in an otherwise civilized world. But in his remarkable book entitled *Hostage*, he writes, "I made the twenty-seventh Psalm a credo for my survival, 'The Lord is my light and my salvation. Whom shall I fear?' I would not be frightened by Hizballah. I should fear only that I might lose my values, my faith. 'One thing I have desired of the Lord, that I should seek: That I may dwell in the house of the Lord all the days of my life.' If I resolved to make my cell the house of the Lord, then I could survive the ordeal."[2]

Next in our David story, we see that his faith comes through with brilliant certainty in the poetic beauty of Psalm 37. Here David's faith takes shape as he says,

> Trust in the LORD, and do good. . . .
> Take delight in the LORD
>   and he will give you the desires of your heart.

> Commit your way to the LORD;
>   trust in him, and he will act.
> Be still before the LORD,
>   and wait patiently for him.

[Ps. 37:3–5, 7]

Drawing on a modern translation, we hear David as he continues, "God has not taken a vacation; he is here. . . . It will take time, but the victory is ultimately God's. Those who live in God's will shall surely discover that his purposes prevail, that true joy and peace and security come from him. Let us wait on God and seek daily to obey him. He is our salvation and our security, and nothing in this world can take that away from us."[3]

It is generally believed that these words were written while David was a fugitive from King Saul, yet his trust and faith are firmly fixed on his ever-present God. How grateful we can be that God is never on vacation.

In the early words of Psalm 57 we sense that David is still on the run as a fugitive. Even though he knows that Saul has a contract out on his life, the closing words of the psalm reflect David's faith, "Your love, O God, is steadfast; Your grace is everlasting. Even when I'm beaten down by depression and ensnared by my weakness and frailties and my own lust threatens to devour me, you are my God and you will not let me go. I am determined to serve you, O Lord. May my life be a continual thank offering to you. I shall sing your praises forever."[4]

The key word in David's psalm of praise is *steadfast*—faithful, determined. It is this kind of faith the apostle Paul had in mind when he wrote to his Christian friends in Corinth, "Therefore, my beloved, be steadfast, immovable, always excelling in the work of the Lord, because you know that in the Lord your labor is not in vain" (1 Cor. 15:58).

The inspired writer of the First Epistle of John caught the spirit of David's faith when he gave us these words, "All of us who are born of God are gaining the victory over the world. It is our faith which gives us the victory."[5]

Another inspiring faith role model moved onto the stage of our biblical story many years before King David's time. Her name was Ruth, the central character in one of the most beautifully crafted short stories in all literature. Ruth was the great-grandmother of David and one of the four women listed in Matthew's genealogy of Jesus.

There are a number of reasons why I find the drama of Ruth a faith challenge. We first meet her in her native land of Moab, and are introduced to her as the wife of one of the sons of a widow named Naomi—Israelite refugees from Judah. According to the story, the wife of Naomi's other son was named Orpah, also a native of Moab.

After several years, both of Naomi's sons had died. This meant that Naomi, Ruth, and Orpah were alone. When Naomi decided to return to her homeland of Judah, her two daughters-in-law started to accompany her. Apparently they had gone just a little way when Naomi, knowing the emotional upheaval of being a stranger in a foreign country, urged Ruth and Orpah to remain in their native land so they could put the pieces of their lives together again in company with their friends and relatives.

According to the storyteller, Orpah did return to her home, but Ruth insisted on staying with her mother-in-law. That is the last we hear of Orpah, but according to certain Jewish legends, Orpah was the great-great-grand-mother of the giant Goliath who terrorized the Israelite army when the Philistines and the Israelites were poised for battle in the valley of Elah. Obviously, we have no proof of that intriguing possibility, but we do know for a fact that Ruth was David's great-grandmother, and we do have the colorful story of David's winning contest over Goliath.

We know from the story that Ruth continued west with Naomi, and the two women made their home among Naomi's old friends and kinfolk in Bethlehem. We know, too, that Ruth abandoned her Moabite gods and put faith in the true God of Israel. After a fascinating chain of events, she married one of Bethlehem's leading citizens, a man named Boaz. In due course Ruth had a son named Obed, the father of Jesse, the father of David the psalmist and Israel's king.

It was Ruth's love for her mother-in-law and her faith in God that held her steady in a foreign land among strange people. And it was Ruth's faith that enabled her to not only make a new life but to become an important figure in Israel's history—important enough, in fact, to be listed as one of Jesus' ancestors, even though she was not a Jew.

More than once as I've traveled in foreign countries where the customs and language are far different from what I understand, I have marveled at the quality of Ruth's love and her implicit faith in a God who accepted her as she was and used her in the fulfillment of his salvation plans.

David's God, Ruth's God, and former hostage David Jacobsen's God is a far cry from the story C. S. Lewis tells about the schoolboy who was asked what he thought God was like. He replied that "as far as he could make out, God was 'the sort of person who is always snooping round to see if anyone is enjoying himself and then trying to stop it.'"[6]

No, the God who has made possible the gift of faith is no snoop or joy-killer. Rather he is the God who is *for* us; the God who so loved us "that he gave his only Son, so that everyone who believes in him may not perish but may have eternal life" (John 3:16).

Pope John Paul II has become a stalwart symbol of faith to Christians—Protestant and Catholic—all over the world. I like this brief message he has given us about faith: "In faith we find the victory that overcomes the world. Because we are united with Jesus and sustained by him, there is no challenge we cannot meet, no difficulty we cannot sustain, no obstacle we cannot overcome for the Gospel. Indeed Christ himself guarantees that 'he who believes in me will also do the works that I do; and greater works than these he will do.' The answer to so many problems is found only in faith—a faith manifested and sustained in prayer."[7]

In spite of these reassurances, we all have our moments when our stream of faith seems to have dried up—when it seems as if our faith is far too small to handle the staggering problems that confront us each day. At such moments I find reassurance in the words of Jesus, "I tell you the truth, *if you have faith as small as a mustard seed*, you can say to this mountain, 'Move from here to there' and it will move. Nothing will be impossible for you" (Matt. 17:20 NIV, italics mine). What wonderful good news!

In these words Jesus used an example very familiar to his listeners. They knew all about mustard seeds and just how little they were. So then Jesus told them—and us— that if we exercise just a little bit, just a speck, of his abundant gift of faith, we can move mountains. *Moving mountains* was a Jewish expression for beating or grinding into powder one's difficulties—reducing them to nothing. As if that wasn't enough, Jesus went on to say that with mustard-seed-sized-faith, nothing is impossible—we can do anything!

Faith is a gift from God, and it is ours to nurture, for as we use it, it will grow. Most certainly, the apostle Paul caught the drift of what Jesus had said about faith when he gave this witness to his brothers and sisters in Christ at the church in Philippi in northern Greece, "I can do all things through Christ which strengtheneth me" (Phil. 4:13 KJV).

In one of his sermons, Dr. Norman Vincent Peale said that these seven words can change your life—"I can do all things through Christ." Dr. Peale went on to say, "If you really get going with those seven words, *really* meaning it, *really* believing it, *really* practicing it; and if anything that isn't good in your life is cast out, your life can be changed."[8]

Patrick Henry was one of the great heroes of the American Revolution. He was also the gifted orator who stood up in the little white church in Richmond, Virginia, and gave his famous "Give me liberty or give me death" speech. Of even greater importance, though, was the fact that Patrick Henry had received the gift of faith, a faith he cherished above all else. These are his words, "My most cherished possession I wish I could leave you is my faith in Jesus Christ, for with him and nothing else you can be happy, but without him and with all else you'll never be happy."

In a similar way my mother's faith is a most cherished possession of mine. From the time when I first accepted Jesus as my Savior at the age of ten until I was an adult of thirty-five, my mother prayed that I would really turn my life completely over to the Lord. Those were wavering and wondering years for me. The day came, though, when my decision was made, and I gave myself fully and without reservation to God. At that moment the Lord vindicated my mother's faith in answer to her prayers and those of my son and friends. I am so glad that my mother lived to see the results of her faith.

Unfortunately, from a human point of view it doesn't always work that way. When I think of my maternal grandmother, Mama Wood, I'm reminded of the Bible's definition of faith as given to us by the writer of the Book of Hebrews, "Now faith is the assurance of things hoped for, the conviction of things not seen" (Heb. 11:1). For many years Mama Wood prayed that her son, my Uncle Roy, would accept Christ as his Savior.

When World War II plunged our world into a fiery conflagration, Uncle Roy was sent overseas without Mama Wood seeing the answer to her prayers. Her faith was unwavering, however, and she gave herself to the work of her church, the First Baptist Church of Uvalde, Texas. Her witness for Christ influenced many people, and while her faith remained firm, she died while Uncle Roy was overseas. What she had "hope for" with Uncle Roy was "not seen."

When the war was over and Uncle Roy came home, his first act was to attend church. It was then he accepted Christ, and for the rest of his life he was a dedicated Christian and an active churchman. Mama Wood's faith was fully justified. God never fails, and we can rest easy in the words of Paul to the Christians in Rome and to Christians in all of time, "We know that all things work together for good for those who love God, who are called according to his purpose" (Rom. 8:28).

9

GOD'S GIFT OF HOPE

What oxygen is to the lungs,
Such is hope for the meaning of life.

Emil Brunner

Our friend Bruce Larson, eloquent pastor and author, several years ago spent a week doing some research at the world-famous Menninger Foundation in Topeka, Kansas. During the course of his various conversations with the Menninger staff, he asked them to identify the most important ingredient in the treatment of their emotionally disturbed patients. "I was told," Bruce Larson writes, "that the entire staff was unanimous in singling out *hope* as the most important factor in treatment. They went on to confess that they don't really know how to give hope to a patient. It is a spiritual and elusive gift."[1]

For those of you who are baseball fans, the name of Casey Stengel, for many years the resourceful manager of the New York Yankees, is legendary. His colorful career has produced many delightful stories and sayings, but I think the most distinctive and descriptive comment ever made about him is this: "He was on good terms with hope." Casey Stengel said *Yes* to hope because he constantly carried with him a vision of a better tomorrow.

Perhaps some of the most electrifying stories of the power of hope to come out of the twentieth century are told by and about prisoners who survived the German concentration camps in the Second World War. Dr. Viktor Frankl, one of Europe's most eminent psychiatrists, was a longtime prisoner in these bestial camps. His father, mother, brother, and wife died in the camps or were victims of the gas ovens. Viktor Frankl, prisoner number 119104, somehow managed to survive even the horrors of Auschwitz.

Dr. Frankl's writings and lectures abound with stories of camp inmates who lost all hope of survival and died while others, one way or another, kept their dreams of a future alive. He insists that any prisoner who lost faith in the future was doomed: "With his loss of belief in the future, he also lost his spiritual hold; he let himself decline and became subject to mental and physical decay." Dr. Frankl adds, "Those who know how close the connection is between the state of mind of a man—his courage and hope, or lack of them—and the state of immunity of his body will understand that the sudden loss of hope and courage can have a deadly affect."[2]

I have to believe that in God's marvelous plan of creation he bestowed upon all people in all of time his gift of hope. It is part of our human condition, but it is up to us to accept and nurture it so it becomes a central fact of our lives.

I remember so well a particular night in my own experience. I had just arrived at the Los Angeles airport on my way home from a speaking engagement. After picking up my car, I headed east toward the mountains I had to cross before reaching Victorville and our home. I hadn't gone far before I was caught in a driving rainstorm. By the time I got into the mountains, the rain was coming down in slanting sheets. Then, without warning, my windshield wipers stopped working. I couldn't see much of anything then, but I managed to ease over onto the shoulder and put on my warning blinkers.

A steady stream of traffic eased past slowly, but nobody stopped. After several minutes of helpless waiting, I pulled on my all-weather coat and climbed out of the car, hoping to flag somebody down. But it didn't work, and I was getting soaked, so I climbed back into the car determined to sit there all night if I had to. I prayed, "Lord, you promised that you'd never leave or forsake me. Now, I just hope you'll be with me no matter how long I have to wait."

A few minutes later a car pulled up beside me, and I heard a man's voice, "May I help you?" I shouted back above the noise of the storm, "I sure hope so. My windshield wipers don't work, and I can't see a thing." With that, a young Mexican man pulled his car off the road, got out, and walked over to where I was sitting. Roy had told me that if I ever had car trouble when I was alone to never get out and not let anybody inside my car, so I was edgy when this young man opened the car door and climbed in. After examining the wipers, he told me that the wiper battery was dead. He then suggested that I lock the car and ride with him into Palmdale where I could phone Roy for help. This seemed to be the only solution, and by this time I felt at ease with him. When we reached Palmdale and the Holiday Inn, my new-found friend let me out, refusing payment for his kindness, and drove off. While waiting for Roy to arrive, I sat quietly and thanked the Lord. Once again I had been assured that if I placed my trust and hope in the Lord, he would hear and answer.

While collecting my thoughts on God's wonderful gift of hope, I was profoundly impressed by a statement made by Vaclav Havel, a playwright and former president of a free and independent Czechoslovakia. Mr. Havel explained what hope means to him, "I am not an optimist because I'm not sure that everything ends well, nor am I a pessimist because I'm not sure that everything ends badly! I just carry hope in my heart. Hope is a feeling that life and work have meaning. You either have it or you don't, regardless of the state of the world around you. Life without hope is an empty, boring, and useless life. I cannot imagine that I could strive for something if I did not carry hope in me. I am thankful to God for this gift. It is as big a gift as life itself."

Hope—a vision of the future—has energized people throughout all of history. And from history and the Bible drama we discover some heroic models of people whose lives were invigorated by hope.

History's classical writers have given us rich descriptive accounts of the short life of Alexander the Great, who was born in 356 B.C. Alexander was the son of King Philip of Macedon, and as a pupil of Aristotle, he received the finest education available at that time. After the death of his father, Alexander succeeded to the throne, and in a few short years he gained acclaim as one of the ablest military technicians of the day. The story is told that on the occasion of his leaving Greece for one of his eastern military campaigns he liberally passed out gifts to his friends and associates. So lavish was his generosity that one of his friends said, "Sir, you've given away so much that you'll have nothing left for yourself." To this Alexander responded, "Oh yes, I have. I still have my hopes." Hope and vision for the future burned brightly for Alexander and brought him the fulfillment of his dreams before his untimely death from a burning fever at the age of thirty-three.

We can learn much from Alexander, but we can learn more, I believe, from the many colorful models of hope and courage who are active in the Bible drama. And among them is a young Jewish woman who showed enormous hope and courage in the crisis moments of her life. Her name was Esther, and her story is told in part in the Book of Esther.

Not once in this amazing Esther story is the name of God mentioned, and the words *hope* and *faith* are conspicuously absent. Yet in Esther we have a striking exhibit of hope and trust as she moves, fearfully at times, toward the fulfillment of her destiny.

Esther—Hadassah—an orphaned Jewish girl in exile in the strange land of ancient Persia, was raised by an older cousin named Mordecai. As with most faithful Jews who were a part of a foreign society many miles from Jerusalem, Mordecai and Esther were likely very familiar with the poetry of the ancient psalmists:

> The LORD is my rock,
> my fortress, and my deliverer.
> [Ps. 18:2]

> For you, O Lord, are my hope, my trust.
> [Ps. 71:5]

Happy are those whose help is the God of Jacob,
whose hope is in the LORD their God.
[Ps. 146:5]

And it is a good thing they were because, according to
the sacred writer, Esther and Mordecai would be put to
an earthshaking test. It seems that King Ahasuerus of Persia had deposed his number one queen because she had
refused to obey an order, and in doing so she had set a
deplorable example for all Persian women. Insubordina-
tion of any description could not be tolerated. To replace
her, a beauty contest was held to find the most beautiful
young woman in all the vast empire of one hundred and
twenty-seven provinces stretching from India to Ethiopia.

With a keen eye for beauty—even that of his own
cousin—Mordecai entered Esther in the contest. Next
we're told that she was judged the most beautiful woman
in all the Persian Empire, and that when the king saw her,
he immediately fell in love with her and made her his
queen. In the apocryphal additions to the Book of Esther,
the writer takes us further behind the scenes and gives us
Mordecai's instructions to Esther as she prepared to
assume her new role, "She was to fear God and keep his
commandments just as she had done when she was with
him. So Esther made no change in her way of life" (Rest
of Esther 2:20 NEB).

After a time, according to the story, jealousy and court
intrigue unleashed a plot to kill all of the Jews in the
empire because Haman, the prime minister, had a bitter
grudge against Mordecai. Through subterfuge Haman
got King Ahasuerus to issue an edict that called for all of
the Jews to be exterminated on a specified day.

When Mordecai read the edict, in frantic desperation
he got word through to Queen Esther that she *must* inter-

vene with the king in order to save not only the lives of thousands of Jews but her own life as well. You see neither King Ahasuerus nor his prime minister knew that the young queen was a Jew, but Mordecai reminded Esther that when her identity was discovered, her life, too, would be in jeopardy.

Esther then reminded her cousin through a note that court protocol prohibited her from going to the throne room without first being invited, and that to do so was at the risk of her life. Mordecai insisted that she chance it, saying, "Perhaps you have come to royal dignity for just such a time as this" (Esther 4:14).

In obedience to all that she hoped and dreamed for her people, Esther decked herself out in all of the splendor of her royal robes and appeared at the door of the king's throne room. Overcome by her manner and beauty, Ahasuerus invited her in and asked what she wanted. In reply, Esther issued an invitation for him and Haman to attend a banquet to be held in her quarters. The king responded to his queen's invitation with enthusiasm.

Esther's banquet must have been a huge success, because during the course of the evening King Ahasuerus asked her to make whatever request she desired and assured her the request would be granted "even to the half of my kingdom" (Esther 5:6). Esther was not ready yet to tip her hand, though, so she issued another invitation for the king and Haman to return the next night for another banquet, and she told them that at that time she would make her request known.

Events unfolded just as Esther had planned, and after the second sumptuous banquet, King Ahasuerus repeated his offer to give Esther whatever she wanted. And this time she bared her soul, and right in front of Haman she revealed his plot to exterminate her and all of her people, the Jews. In a rage the king disposed of Haman and agreed to a plan that would prevent the mass slaughter of the Jews.

Esther, the Jewish queen of Persia, had earned her place in history because of her devotion to the God of Israel. Esther's faith and hope, coupled with her courage, inspire us to be hope-filled Christians in our alien and sometimes precarious world.

To celebrate the deliverance of all of the Jews in Persia and the one hundred and twenty-seven provinces across the ancient near-eastern world that were controlled by the Persian king, the festival of Purim, the most joyous of all Jewish holidays, was established by Mordecai and Esther.

To this day it is celebrated by faithful Jews all around the world one month before Passover. While it is a most joyous and spirited holiday, it has its serious dimension as well for it encourages the Jews to cling to their hopes and never despair in spite of the "Hamans" that may move onto the world scene. The saga of Esther, one of our noblest spiritual ancestors, is an inspiration of hope and courage to God's people in all of time.

In fact, Esther reminds me of how I felt at a time of crisis many years ago. My life wasn't in peril as Esther's was, but I felt my self-esteem and reputation were on the line. The event I am thinking of occurred during the years our television program was on the air.

The producer of our show came to me one day with a problem related to a specific episode in one of the shows. "Dale," he said, "we need a Sunday school kind of chorus for Sherri Jackson [who was a little girl at the time] to sing to her father. We just can't find anything suitable in public domain. Could you write one that would fit into the episode?"

I indicated I was willing to try and asked how much time I had to come up with something. In reply, Jack Lacy said, "Twenty minutes." Completely aghast, I said, "There's just no way I can come up with even the simplest of choruses in just twenty minutes." Quietly Jack responded to my near hysteria, "Try!"

I closed the door of my Samuel Goldwyn Studios dressing room and prayed, "Lord, I have faith in your ability to do anything. Now, you know we need an appropriate little chorus. We desperately need just the right thing to be the kind of witness we want to make. My *hope* and faith are in you. Please give me just the right words and tune."

Suddenly, Paul's words from the thirteenth chapter of First Corinthians flashed into my consciousness—faith, hope, and charity. And wonder of wonders, in twenty minutes' time I had the words and music to "Have Faith, Hope, and Charity, That's the Way to Live Successfully. How Do I Know? The Bible Tells Me So." I tried it out on the cast. They liked it, and we closed the show with it.

When the sponsor and network people saw the show, they said my chorus was too religious, and the producer was instructed to delete it on reruns. However, Don Cornell of the Lucky Strike Hit Parade heard it and asked for permission to record it. It was an immediate hit, and "The Bible Tells Me So" remained on the Hit Parade for weeks. God had his way—my hopes prevailed!

The second model of hope that emerges like a thunder clap from the Bible story is none other than the apostle Paul. In fact, I believe Paul could well be labeled "The Apostle of Hope." To chart Paul's travels and activities throughout all of his life from the moment of his conversion on the Damascus road is to picture years of bone-grinding travel on foot throughout Asia Minor and Greece and by ship on the turbulent waters of the eastern Mediterranean Sea. In those days there was no such thing as first class travel or comfortable hotel accommodations. Paul's land travel involved walking across open country or on the rock-paved Roman roads, and he would have slept out in the open under the stars, plagued by gnats and mosquitoes. But in spite of the hardship, he remained ruggedly determined to travel anywhere and by whatever means possible to share the Good News of salvation through Christ with people who had not heard it before.

Yet there was more. Paul's world was Roman and pagan. The people worshiped a pantheon of gods and goddesses, but in addition they were required to worship the Roman emperor—not to do so was a crime against the state. This simply meant that Paul's message of one God and salvation through Christ only met with official opposition wherever he went.

In writing to his Christian friends in Corinth, Paul called their attention to his beatings and prison experiences:

> Five times I received from the Jews the forty lashes minus one. Three times I was beaten with rods, once I was stoned, three times I was shipwrecked, I spent a night and a day in the open sea, I have been constantly on the move. I have been in danger from rivers, in danger from bandits, in danger from my own countrymen, in danger from Gentiles. . . . I have labored and toiled and have often gone without sleep; I have known hunger and thirst and have often gone without food; I have been cold and naked.
>
> [2 Cor. 11:24–27 NIV]

Yet it was this same Paul who ranked hope right along with faith and love as the supreme Christian virtues. (See 1 Cor. 13:13.) This same Paul also sent this marvelous benediction to his Christian friends in the imperial city of Rome, "May the God of hope fill you with all joy and peace by your faith in him, until, by the power of the Holy Spirit, you overflow with hope" (Rom. 15:13 NEB). *Overflow with hope!* That is our calling as Christians as the twentieth century winds down to its last hours. I firmly believe that we are to overflow with hope not as a means of escape from the here and now. Rather, our hope engages us in the concerns and needs of the present.

Yes, the social and political world is in a painful upheaval. As I write more than forty wars are raging in remote areas of planet earth—people are dying from starvation by the thousands and from fiery missiles launched by unknown and known foes. As Christians, though, we are not to be harbingers of pessimism and doom. Rather, we are to celebrate God's gift of hope with joy unspeakable and full of glory.

Dr. Viktor Frankl, who I quoted earlier, said somewhere that "survivors were people who believed they were unfinished with life." Because of God's gift of hope, we— you and I—are survivors never finished with life. Hymnwriter and poet Isaac Watts caught the spirit of this when he wrote these electrifying words:

> O God, our help in ages past,
> Our hope for years to come,
> Our shelter from the stormy blast,
> And our eternal home.

> O God, our help in ages past,
> Our hope for years to come,
> Be thou our guide while life shall last,
> And our eternal home.

10

Say Yes to
GOD'S GIFT OF LOVE

The great tragedy of life
is not that men perish
but that they cease to love.

W. Somerset Maugham

"Follow the way of love and eagerly desire spiritual gifts" (1 Cor. 14:1 NIV).

In this statement, the apostle Paul speaks of *the way* of love. However, it isn't straining our purpose here to recognize love as a gift from God to everyone who believes in him. Most certainly, the writer of the First Epistle of John (considered by the earliest Christians and many scholars today to be none other than John the beloved disciple, who also wrote the Gospel of John) seemed to make this point clear when he wrote, "Love is from God; everyone who loves is born of God. . . . God is love" (1 John 4:7–8).

In fact, as we move through the Bible drama from the earliest pages to the end, we have a vivid portrayal of a God who *is* love and who loves. And it was this same Creator-God who shaped human beings in his image who is described by the Gospel writer in these words, "For God so loved the world that he gave his only Son, so that everyone who believes in him may not perish but may have eternal life" (John 3:16). Most assuredly, the gift of love is ours, but the appropriation and expression of that gift is up to us. It is what we do with it that makes the difference.

Sue Monk Kidd is the gifted writer of a delightful book entitled *God's Joyful Surprise*. In it she has some inspired words on God's gift of love: "The joyful experience of being loved by God makes it impossible for us to separate loving God from loving others. No matter how we express our love for one another, we may be sure that God will multiply His presence to us. For we are nearest God when we love."[1]

Unfortunately, because of the plethora of writing on the subject of love, we may fail to catch its full significance due to overfamiliarity. For that reason it is important that we take a second look at a statement John included in his First Epistle, "Love must not be a matter of words or talk; it must be genuine, *and show itself in action* (1 John 3:18 NEB, italics mine). This is a momentous truth; Christian love is not a feeling or an emotion. Rather, it is an act of the will; it is something as John says, *that we do*. It is what we *are*, and it makes a difference in how we act and even how we look.

The apostle Paul is the author of a most beautiful and perceptive poetic essay on the subject of love. When he wrote those paragraphs (preserved for us in the thirteenth chapter of First Corinthians) to his Christian friends in the pagan Greek city of Corinth, he laid himself right on the line. These folks knew the human Paul. He had lived with them, and they had seen him under stress. No, he was not perfect, but, yes, they knew he loved God and he loved them. Paul didn't have to apologize for anything he said in those paragraphs about what it means to love, and I have to believe that his inner feelings of love and his outer actions of love were clearly visible to everyone he met.

In one of his books Frederick Buechner comments that Paul certainly wasn't much to look at, and he quotes a few sentences from the apocryphal *Acts of Paul and Thecla* that were written several years after Paul's death. In this book Paul is described as "baldheaded, bowlegged, strongly built, a man small in size, with meeting eyebrows, with a rather large nose." That is certainly not a particularly flattering physical description, but the payoff comes in the conclusion when the ancient writer adds that "at times he looked like a man, and at times he had the face of an angel."[2] It seems clear that it was Paul's love in action as expressed in his writing and preaching that even made the difference in his appearance as described here.

Paul knew all about the distorted notion of love that was prevalent and that was characteristic of pagan thinking and action in ancient Corinth. He had to have been keenly aware of the temple of Aphrodite that loomed high above the city on the Acrocorinth. It was there that a thousand temple prostitutes entertained in religious orgies, making a mockery of authentic love.

Consequently, it is most significant that Paul, with a magnificent economy of words, lists once and for all for his Corinthian Christian friends what it means to act out authentic love:

Love is patient; love is kind; love is not envious or boast-
ful or arrogant or rude. It does not insist on its own way;
it is not irritable or resentful; it does not rejoice in wrong-
doing, but rejoices in the truth. It bears [puts up with]
all things, believes all things, hopes all things, endures
all things.

[1 Cor. 13:4–7]

These are all action words—they all speak of something
we are or something we do. There is nothing soft and sen-
timental or licentious in Paul's step-by-step description
of love.

At times we might wish that Paul had been a little less
specific when he wrote these words. For example, being
patient and *kind* doesn't come easily for most of us as we
make our way through the give-and-take of each twenty-
four-hour day. William Barclay commented somewhere
in his writings that so much of Christianity is good but
unkind. How sad, if true. I suspect it is true, though, as
I read and hear about the attacks of some Christians
against those who see and interpret their faith differently.
Division and disunity are dreadful blights on the teachings of Jesus about love.

By contrast, in writing to the Christians in Colossae
Paul gave them and us this powerful love-model, "You are
God's chosen people. He loves you and has made you holy.
So you must be tender-hearted, kind, humble, gentle, and
patient. Bear with one another. If you have reason to com-
plain against someone, forgive him. The Lord forgave you,
so you must forgive others. Above all, love one another.
Love makes everything work in perfect harmony."[3]

At this point, we have to ask, "Where did Paul get this
kind of insight? What was his authority for this kind of
demanding lifestyle?" After all, before his conversion he

had been a rigid and law-abiding Pharisee who was very familiar with the Jewish Creed as spelled out in what he knew as the Shema, the opening words of which are, "Hear, O Israel, the LORD is our God, one LORD, and you must love the LORD your God with all your heart and soul and strength" (Deut. 6:4–5 NEB).

Paul at that time knew that *love* was a dominant theme throughout all of the Book of Deuteronomy. His rigid understanding of that ancient Law, however, obliged him to love only those who interpreted the Law precisely the way he and his fellow Pharisees did. For Paul at that time, his way was the *right* way, and he had been willing to imprison and even kill those who believed differently.

After Paul's conversion to Christ, the way of love took on a deeper and more profound dimension. Undoubtedly, those disciples of Jesus who had been present at the time of his discussion with a certain lawyer had told Paul how Jesus answered the question as to which commandment was the most important. In all probability it was Peter who explained that Jesus had quoted for the lawyer the words from Deuteronomy—words that would have been very familiar to him. Then, in addition, Paul learned that Jesus added a second commandment to the first, "Love your neighbour as yourself" (Mark 12:31 NEB; see also Matt. 22:34–40; Luke 10:25–28).

Paul also would have been told that Jesus followed his recitation of these two commandments with the words, "There is no other commandment greater than these." Wrapped up in these two commandments is the kind of action we are to take with God's gift of love. Here is our model for love of family, of friends, of other Christians, of everybody—every day and always. It is practical, uncomplicated, and straight to the point. We are to love

God and express that love in everything we do. We are to love and respect ourselves as people created in the image of God, and we are to love other people with the same degree of intensity that we rightly love ourselves. Peter put it this way, "Above all, keep your love for one another at full strength, because love cancels innumerable sins" (1 Peter 4:8 NEB).

Dr. Eugene Kennedy, the thoughtful and perceptive Christian sociologist and interpreter of love helps us at this point. He writes, "Love always brings us back to the same point of reference. A man must learn to love himself properly if he is to love others at all. This learning is hard because it demands that he sacrifice himself in the process . . . love takes root as a man becomes increasingly sensitive to others and the effect he has on them. . . . When we are insensitive to ourselves, we can only blunder through life, hurting others even when we do not realize it, leaving the scarred and broken trail that follows always in the wake of rudeness and selfishness."[4]

There is an important thought here that needs to be emphasized. In the past, at least among certain Christians, there has been the tendency to denigrate ourselves in the name of piety, but this sells both God and ourselves short.

In writing to Gentile Christians in Asia Minor, Peter insisted, "You are God's own people. Tell all the world the wonderful things God has done for you. . . . Once you were 'nobody.' . . . But you have found Christ and now you are 'God's people.'"[5] To be sure, it was God's gift of love that lifted us from being nobody to becoming God's people.

In concluding his marvelous essay on love, Paul summed up all that he had said with these words, "Faith, hope, and love, these three last forever. But the greatest of them all is love."[6] In other words, "Great as faith and hope are, love is still greater. Faith without love is cold, and hope without love is grim. Love is the fire which kindles faith and it is the light which turns hope into certainty."[7]

Throughout our reflections so far on the *gift* and *way* of love no attempt has been made to qualify or explain the use of our English word *love*. The truth of the matter is that for many people today the word *love* is the most abused and confused word in our language. We *love* everything from pizza and our new Buick to the latest soap opera on television.

Tragically, our rather flippant use of the word *love* has stripped it of the passion and intensity that Paul was trying to get across in his Corinthian letter. We are indebted to Professor Elton Trueblood for some helpful thinking on what Paul was actually saying. He suggests that the Greek word Paul used, which translators have rendered *charity* and *love*, has almost no English equivalent. In today's world *charity* refers to forms of philanthropy, and as has already been suggested, so often the word *love* has been over-sentimentalized and trivialized in modern literature and advertising.

Drawing on the suggestion of an English philosopher, Dr. Trueblood endorses the idea that "caring" is "as yet an unspoiled term" and that it is more expressive of Paul's deepest meaning. With this thought in mind, Paul's opening sentence in First Corinthians 13 would read, "If I speak in the tongues of mortals and of angels, but do not care, I am a noisy gong or a clanging cymbal." And verse 8 would open with these words, "Caring never ends."[8]

The meaning of the word *love* as Jesus used it and about which the apostle Paul wrote is passionate and selfless caring. Reflection on this thought throws two vivid pictures onto the screen of my mind. I have written earlier in *Angel Unaware* the story of our little Robin, our Down's syndrome baby. At one point I asked the doctor what Roy and I should do to provide Robin with the best possible care during the time she would be with us.

The doctor's response has been forever etched in my memory, "Take her home and love her. Love will help more than anything else in a situation like this—more than all the hospitals and all the medical science in the world." At that time the doctors were just beginning to talk about the power of tender, loving care as a therapeutic response to illness in the healing process.

The second picture on my mind's screen goes way back to my childhood in central Texas. Christmas was such a joy-filled time in our family as we came together to celebrate the birth of Christ. As children we were, of course, always excited over the exchange of gifts. In looking back now I know that the most precious gift we had was our love for one another. As I wrote in an earlier book, "Is this not the true Christmas? Isn't that what Jesus came to accomplish—'A new commandment I give unto you, That ye love one another. . . .' At least in those first childhood Christmases we began to learn that lesson of love. The gifts were secondary; the greatest gift of all was the plain, simple, gift of love."[9]

NOTES

Chapter 1   Say *Yes* to God's Gift of Tomorrow

1. Norman Vincent Peale, "Give Me Tomorrow" (Pawling, N.Y.: Foundation for Christian Living, 1975).

2. Paul Tournier, *The Meaning of Persons* (New York: Harper & Row, 1957), 218.

3. Peale, "Give Me Tomorrow."

4. Frank C. Laubach, *The Inspired Letters* (New York: Thomas Nelson & Sons, 1956), 104, Gal. 6:9–10, italics mine.

5. *Wings of Healing* (San Francisco: Grace Cathedral Ministry of Healing, 1942), 39.

Chapter 2   Say *Yes* to God's Gift of Change and Growth

1. Bruce Larson, *The Meaning and Mystery of Being Human* (Waco: Word Books, 1978), 69–70.

2. Michael Marshall, *A Change of Heart* (London: Collins Liturgical Publications, 1981), 18.

3. Marshall, *A Change of Heart*, 20.

4. Paul Tournier, *Learn to Grow Old* (New York: Harper & Row, 1972), 192.

5. Dorothy L. Sayers, *The Mind of the Maker* (Westport, Conn: Greenwood Press, 1971).

6. Evelyn Underhill, *Concerning Inner Life and the House of the Soul* (New York: Methuen, 1947).

7. Ben Campbell Johnson, *The Heart of Paul* (Waco: Word Books, 1976), 92, 2 Cor. 5:16–17, italics mine.

8. Floyd and Harriett Thatcher, *Long Term Marriage* (Waco: Word Books, 1980), 169.

9. Samuel H. Miller, *The Life of the Soul* (New York: Harper & Row, 1951), 17.

Chapter 3   Say *Yes* to God's Gift of Joy and Laughter

1. An excerpt from an old pamphlet originally published by Epworth Press; Elton Trueblood, *The Humor of Christ* (New York: Harper & Row, 1964).

2. Olaf M. Norlie, *The New Testament—A New Translation in Modern English* (Grand Rapids: Zondervan, 1961), Ps. 16:11.

3. James A. Michener, *The World Is My Home* (New York: Random House, 1992), 496.

4. Quoted on the jacket of *I Stand By the Door, the Life of Sam Shoemaker*, Helen Shoemaker (Waco: Word Books, 1967).

5. William Barclay, *The Gospel of Matthew, vol. 1*, rev. ed. (Philadelphia: Westminster Press, 1975), 88.

6. Harold Kushner, *When All You've Ever Wanted Isn't Enough* (New York: Pocket Books, 1986).

7. Fulton J. Sheen, *Treasure in Clay—The Autobiography of Fulton J. Sheen* (Garden City, N. Y.: Doubleday, 1980).

Chapter 4   Say *Yes* to God's Gift of Prayer

1. Henri J. M. Nouwen, *Reaching Out* (Garden City, N.J.: Doubleday & Company, Inc., 1975), 90.

2. James C. Houston, *The Transforming Friendship* (Oxford: Lion Publishing Co., 1989), 3.

3. William Barclay, *The Gospel of Luke* (Philadelphia: Westminster Press, 1975), 143.

4. Samuel M. Shoemaker, *And Thy Neighbor* (Waco: Word Books, 1967).

5. Norman Vincent Peale, "The World's Greatest Power," PLUS (Pawling, N.Y.: Peale Center for Christian Living, March 1992).

6. Paul S. Rees, *Don't Sleep through the Revolution* (Waco: Word Books, 1969).

Chapter 5   Say *Yes* to God's Gift of Wonder

1. Leslie F. Brandt, *Psalms/Now* (St. Louis: Concordia, 1973), 17, Ps. 8.

2. Brandt, *Psalms/Now*, 17.

3. Carl Sagan, "A Little Blue Dot," *Parade Magazine*, September 9, 1990.

4. Brandt, *Psalms/Now*, 17.

5. Leslie D. Weatherhead, *Key Next Door* (Nashville: Abingdon Press, 1939).

6. Frederick Buechner, *Telling the Truth* (San Francisco: Harper & Row, 1977), 66.

Chapter 6   Say *Yes* to God's Gift of Friendship

1. Martin E. Marty, *Friendship* (Allen, Tex.: Argus Communications, 1980), 98.

2. Leslie D. Weatherhead, *Key Next Door* (Nashville: Abingdon Press, 1939), 37.

3. M. Scott Peck, *The Road Less Traveled* (New York: Simon & Schuster, 1978).

4. Allen Emory, *Turtle on a Fencepost* (Waco: Word Books, 1979).

Chapter 7   Say *Yes* to God's Gift of Risk and Difficulty

1. Mark O. Hatfield, *Between a Rock and a Hard Place* (Waco: Word Books, 1976), 90–99.

2. C. S. Lewis, *Mere Christianity* (New York: Macmillan, 1943), 171.

3. Paul Tournier, *Learn to Grow Old* (New York: Harper & Row, 1972).

4. Paul Tournier, *The Meaning of Persons* (New York: Harper & Row, 1957), 206.

5. Alan Jones, *Passion for the Pilgrimage* (San Francisco: Harper & Row, 1989), 107.

6. John Knox, *Jesus, Lord and Christ* (New York: Harper & Brothers, 1958), 118.

7. Floyd Thatcher, *The Miracle of Easter* (Waco: Word Books, 1980), 19.

Chapter 8   Say *Yes* to God's Gift of Faith

1. Leslie F. Brandt, *Psalms/Now* (St. Louis: Concordia, 1973), 43.

2. David Jacobsen with Gerald Astor, *Hostage: My Nightmare in Beirut* (New York: Donald I. Fine, 1991), 107.

3. Brandt, *Psalms/Now*, 59.

4. Brandt, *Psalms/Now*, 93.

5. Frank C. Laubach, *The Inspired Letters* (New York: Thomas Nelson & Sons, 1956), 214, 1 John 5:4.

6. C. S. Lewis, *Mere Christianity* (New York: Macmillan, 1943), 69.

7. Pope John Paul II, *The Things of the Spirit*, ed. Kathryn Spink (San Francisco: Harper & Row, 1982), 23–24.

8. Norman Vincent Peale, "Seven Words Can Change Your Life" (Pawling, N. Y.: Foundation for Christian Living, 1976).

Chapter 9   Say *Yes* to God's Gift of Hope

1. Bruce Larson, *There's a Lot More to Health Than not Being Sick* (Waco: Word Books, 1981), 90.

2. Viktor E. Frankl, *Man's Search for Meaning* (Boston: Beacon Press, 1959), 74–75.

Chapter 10   Say *Yes* to God's Gift of Love

1. Sue Monk Kidd, *God's Joyful Surprise* (San Francisco: Harper & Row, 1987), 242.

2. Frederick Buechner, *Peculiar Treasures* (San Francisco: Harper & Row, 1979), 128, 133.

3. Frank C. Laubach, *The Inspired Letters*, Col. 3:12–14, italics mine.

4. Eugene C. Kennedy, *A Time for Love* (Garden City, N.Y.: Doubleday, 1970), 116–117.

5. Laubach, *Inspired Letters*, 1 Pet. 2:9–10.

6. Laubach, *Inspired Letters*, 1 Cor. 13:13.

7. William Barclay, *The Letters to the Corinthians* (Philadelphia: Westminster Press, 1975), 126.

8. Elton Trueblood, *The Yoke of Christ* (New York: Harper & Row, 1958).

9. Dale Evans Rogers, *Christmas Always* (Old Tappan, N. J.: Fleming H. Revell, 1958), 19.